JUST *Being* ME

TAUNYA
LYNNETTE

Just Being Me

Editor: JenWestWriting Editing & Marketing Services

Cover designed by: Dzine By Kellie

Cover photos by: Lindria Dockett Photography

Typesetter: Leslie Allen of All-EN Ventures LLC

Printed in the United States of America

Published by
TLS Media Group LLC
P.O. Box 6683
Largo, MD 20792
Taunya@TLSMediaGroup.com
www.taunyalynette.com

This is a work of creative non-fiction. The events are of the author's life and experiences. All the stories in this book are true and told solely from the author's perspective.

ISBN: 978-1-7342696-0-4
ISBN: 978-1-7342696-1-1 (e-book)

Dedication

I dedicate this book to my mother, brother, and in memory of my beloved father.

TABLE OF CONTENTS

INTRODUCTION

Just Being Me is a book designed to inspire you to be the very best you can be, no matter what the situation is. This is to all women who encourage themselves every day, knowing and believing that they can do all things through Christ that strengthens them. If you have been singled out for how you look or because of your race gender, this book is for you.

If you are the only woman on the job in a male-dominated field, this book is for you. If you are the only woman at the board meeting, and if you are excluded from the happy hour invites because the majority of your co-workers are male, it's okay. If you stand up for yourself, if you are your own boss, if you are working a nine-to-five and have a side hustle, if someone told you that you can't do something and didn't have the guts to tell you why, but you did it anyway and conquered it, then this book is for you.

I wrote this book hoping that it would inspire you not to allow other people to tell you what you can't do, not to be afraid, but to have the courage to speak up and stand up for what you believe. Once you make up your mind to do something, do it. Don't wait for someone else to encourage you to do something. If your instincts are telling you to do it, then do it.

For the past seven years, I have been writing inspirational articles for women. I always wondered what effect my articles would have on the readers and if they inspired or encouraged them in some way.

When I'm writing, I always say what I feel. No filters, no special answers or responses; you just get me. I'm just being me. I am not a doctor or psychiatrist; I just speak from experience or what I have been exposed to. Now, it may not be for everybody, but it's definitely for people that have been through something.

This book is relatable in real-life situations, meaning whatever is going on in your life, what could be holding you back from doing something can be overcome if you put your mind to it.

When writing this book, I wanted to share inspiring words and some of my life stories that can help you have the courage to stand up for yourself and encourage yourself without waiting on someone else to help you. I wanted to tell you that if you get out of your comfort zone, fear will fail, and you will win.

Just Being Me is a guide to not allowing stress to take over your life. Do you know you could be stressed and not realize it? Well, I will talk about symptoms of stress and what to do to prevent it.

Just Being Me is an aid to you being teachable. Are you supporting everyone else's dream and not yours? I will talk about investing in yourself, which is a must-do if you wish to succeed in this world.

Just Being Me is a navigation system through losing a loved one. Grief is a journey; I am going to talk about ways to help you deal with it and move on with your life while still honoring your loved one.

Just Being Me is a guide to taking care of yourself. My body is my temple and I will take care of it. What about you? Are you doing things to make yourself sick? Are you happy about how you look? Are you experiencing any pain in unusual places and not doing anything about it? I am going to tell you what happened to me and why you need to act on anything physical that is not normal and bothering you.

Just Being Me is learning how to get along with family, learning how to forgive and being able to honor your parents and take care of them when needed. Family: you love them; at least most of them. But what do you do with the ones that get on your nerves or the ones that are causing drama in the family? Are you a family member who is passing off negative feedback to other family members? Do you have a problem with a family member and don't know what to do? I am going to talk about that. I love my family, but sometimes people say things, and you have to kindly respond in a respectable way that won't lead to a fight or an argument.

Just Being Me is all about me telling you what I think of the situation, and maybe what I think or what I did in a similar situation will work in your favor as well.

Just Being Me is learning how to turn your obstacles into opportunities. Obstacles are not the end of the world, but they are the path to new opportunities once you see the bigger picture.

Just Being Me is learning how to be unbreakable and strong, while at the same time, knowing that you can't always do things on your own, and you are not ashamed to ask for help if needed.

Just Being Me is becoming a better person. You're not perfect, but you are better than you were last year.

I'm sure you are wondering, "Why this book?" *Just Being Me* covers various areas in a person's life. It's not in any special order as to when things can happen. You never know what is going to happen in your life; you just have to be ready, so get ready and figure out what to do.

Each chapter topic is a reflection of something that I have experienced in life, and it is really me just being me. I believe others have experienced some of the things that I discussed and maybe are still going through something and trying to figure out what to do. I hope that my words will inspire you to be confident and make the right decisions in your life and not allow other people or situations to take over or stop you from doing what you need to do.

I believe the experiences that I share in between some of my life stories are relatable. I'm sure you want to get over what you are experiencing, move on, and take things to the next level. This book will give you a good feeling and empower you to live your best life. This book will inspire all women of all ages and backgrounds with hopes that it will guide you through any situation that comes your way.

Women are often the glue that holds everyone together, both at work and at home. Inspire yourself to reach greater heights. Take care of yourself and your mental, emotional and physical health because you can't do anything if you're sick. Overcome personal and professional obstacles and achieve your dreams because dreams do come true!

CHAPTER 1

Nothing Can Stop Me

Saying "nothing can stop me" is like never giving up. Whatever you are doing or whatever you desire to do, never give up on your dreams. Has someone ever told you that you can't do something, or you won't amount to anything? Some people just speak negatively, but you can't allow other people to direct your path. Don't let anything or anyone get you down.

When I started my career in information technology, there were a lot of negative people telling me that I shouldn't do this type of work and that I was never going to get ahead. I remember a male friend telling me that no one would hire me in this field because they didn't want a woman doing this work. The fact was they didn't think a woman could do the job. I would often get that reaction from my male counterparts, but that didn't stop me. I continued working in the field of Information technology and have made it my career. It has not been easy, but it was something that I was interested in from early on, and I became passionate about technology and the inner workings of it. I don't know what I would be doing if I had listened to others. I never allowed anyone to dictate what they thought I should do; I've always made my own decisions. As I have matured, I have grown spiritually, and when I am considering a change, I pray and talk it over with God.

"Nothing can stop me" is the mindset of not allowing others to smash your dreams; it's being determined to go out and do your own thing without excuses. "Nothing can stop me" is not letting life just pass you by. If you want to start a revolution, then do it! If you want to sing or act, then do it! "Nothing can stop me" is believing in yourself; believing that you can go all the way. If you have a dream, then you go for it. "Nothing can stop me" is about having the courage to keep on trying and never giving up. If you allow someone to take over your life, then you are giving in. Set your goals high, and don't stop until you get there. It may not happen when you want it, but it will come as long as you stick to it.

"Nothing can stop me" is having that dream to do whatever it is you want to do and being able to make the changes in your life to make the dreams come true. As you're reading this book today, make the change in your life so that your dreams will come true. Be determined to execute a plan of action. Even if you think that it may be difficult, make a plan to do it. While making your plan, you can write down the steps it will take to execute and work your plan, step by step until you get it done.

Being determined means wanting to do something and not allowing anyone else or any difficulties to stop you. You can be determined to earn a college degree; to do that, you would need to complete a college degree program at a school of your choice. A difficulty could be not having enough money to pay for college. So, you can come up with ways to get the funds. A few examples to conquer this would be to get a part-time job, work full-time and go to school at night, or apply for a school loan. All of these ideas would give you an option to work toward your degree. It may take longer, but it can be accomplished. Problems are not stop signs; they are guidelines to prepare you for your next challenge.

"Nothing can stop me" is never giving up. Never stop believing in yourself. Never stop fighting for what you believe.

As a single woman, there are things that I want to do, but sometimes my friends can't do it or participate. They have other responsibilities, or sometimes they may not have the finances to do so. I remember my cousin Blanche telling me that if I want to do something and I desire to do it, then I should do it while I still can. Every day is not promised; you don't know what your situation will be a year from now or in the future, and you don't know what your friend's situation would be, so if you desire to do something, see something or go somewhere, then you should go. I love to travel, and I love to be active and do things without waiting on people to do it. That talk I had with my cousin Blanche inspired me. She was right, and since that talk we had, I have been traveling all over the world. There have been times that I have traveled solo, but I have also travelled with a few of my cousins. The key to traveling solo is that you need to be careful of your surroundings and travel to places where there are activities and things to do.

How many of us start out doing something and then we get a little frustrated because things aren't happening fast enough for us and we feel the need to give up? Well, let me tell you, if you have a plan to do something and it appears things are moving too slowly, don't stop! Continue to do what you started. It doesn't matter how long it takes; just don't stop. If you decided to go back to school and get your degree, it may take four to five years or maybe a little longer depending on things happening in your life. Just don't stop.

Set your goals high and don't stop until you get there. I have dreams, and to make them come true, I need to do what it takes to execute them. For example, if I desire to become a best-selling author, I first need to write a book of interest to people and then develop a marketing strategy to sell the book. The book won't sell itself; people have to know about the book to purchase it. So, in order for me to become a best-selling author, I would need to execute a few tasks to make that happen. You have to set your goals, and don't stop until you get there.

If you're determined to stand, nothing can move you. If you're determined to move, nothing can stop you. Determination is the key; it is the act of coming to a decision and having the firmness of purpose. When you are determined, it is like settling a purpose, and nothing can stop you from achieving your purpose. Once you make up your mind to do something, you are determined to see it through to the end.

When you are consistently doing what you need to do to succeed with total focus and resolve, it is incredibly difficult. There is always some type of distraction to get us off-track from what we are trying to accomplish. The ability to work hard and respond positively to failure and adversity is so very crucial. Willpower and determination help us work hard and stick to our ultimate goals.

Nothing can stop you when you allow the past to be the past. Let your past be exactly what it is; it does not define your future. The past is valuable. You learn from your mistakes as well as other people's mistakes, then you let it go! Move on! If something bad happened to you or you made some bad decisions, see it as an opportunity to learn something you didn't know. The past is just like training; you learned from it, you have moved on, and now you know how to handle the situation better or whatever the case may be.

Nothing can stop you if you see your life and future as totally within your control. Allowing yourself to be in total control is having control over your mindset and the way you think. Many people feel luck has a lot to do with success or failure. They think that if you succeed, luck favored you, and if you failed, then luck was against you. Most successful people feel like luck played some role in their success. I don't believe in luck; I believe in faith, and if you have a plan and keep the faith, God will see you through. I personally don't wait for luck or worry about bad luck. If it was meant to be it will be, and if it's part of the plan, then it will happen. It may not come when I want it, but it will come.

Learn to ignore the things you don't have any control over. For some, it's politics, for others, it's family or maybe even global warming. Whatever it is, do what you can do. If you don't like who is in office, go vote. If you can't help your family or friends, just listen and hear them out. If you want to help save the earth, try recycling and reducing your carbon footprint. Be your own change; don't try to make everyone else change. You can only control what's going on in your life, not everyone else's.

Celebrate the success of others; don't resent it. Resentment sucks up a lot of negative energy that can be applied elsewhere. When your friends or family members do something awesome, that doesn't exclude you from doing something awesome. Where success is concerned, you have heard the saying, "birds of a feather flock together," so hang out with your successful friends and family. Get closer to them. You may be able to learn something from them that will help you get to your next level. Don't resent their awesomeness; instead, create and celebrate their awesomeness, and before you know it, you will be celebrating yourself.

Stop complaining, criticizing, and whining; your words have power over you. Whining about your problems will make things worse. If something is wrong, don't waste time complaining about it. Put the energy into making the situation better. Fix it now! Don't talk about what's wrong; talk about how you'll make it better. Do the same with your friends and family—don't serve as a shoulder to cry on or allow them to talk about others in a negative way in your presence. Real friends help their friends make their lives better. I am going to talk more about friendship in a later chapter.

Nothing can stop you. Don't focus on others; just do you! Don't worry about what other people are doing or what they have, such as their cars, clothes, spouses, and jobs. Just focus on your accomplishments. Don't worry about what people think of you. Some may pretend to like you for various reasons aside from you being yourself. They may be superficial, phony, smiling in your face, and talking about you behind your back. Genuine relationships make you happier, and you'll form a genuine relationship when you stop trying to impress others and just be yourself.

Nothing can stop you when you constantly revisit your long-term goals. Create reminders such as a vision board that has pictures of everything you would like to do. It can be something as simple as a photo of you when you were at your ideal weight, and you are currently trying to get back to that place and loose the sixty pounds that you have gained over the years. A reminder can be one or two photos of your family members next to your computer at work to remind you who you really work for.

Every night, take a moment to count your blessings and thank God for what you do have. Whether it's good health, a roof over your head or food in your refrigerator, be thankful for the things you do have. Nothing can stop you from achieving your goals if you have a deeply driven and persistent desire to do something.

Chapter One- *Food for thought* *Nothing Can Stop Me*

What is stopping you from living your dreams?

List your goals and steps that you can do to accomplish them.

CHAPTER 2

Courage

"YOU CAN DO IT:"

RESTORING SELF ESTEEM AND CONFIDENCE

Self-esteem is the opinion we have of ourselves. Everyone lacks confidence sometimes, but people with low self-esteem are unhappy or unsatisfied with themselves most of the time. Low self-esteem may cause problems such as depression and anxiety. Self-esteem deals with how we judge our own worth. High self-esteem enables us to look upon ourselves with value.

There are various causes of low self-esteem. An unhappy childhood, where parents or other significant people such as teachers or coaches were extremely critical, can lead to low self-esteem in an adult. Another cause is poor academic performance in school, resulting in a lack of confidence or a belief that one just does not measure up to others. Later in life, stressful life events such as relationship breakdowns or ongoing financial trouble can negatively affect an adult's self-esteem.

Low self-esteem comes in many forms, each with different signs. Some women with low self-esteem act as if they are happy and successful when they are actually afraid of failure. Perfectionism, procrastination and competitiveness are all signs of this type of low self-esteem. Other women with low self-esteem might act defiantly, as if the rules do not apply to them or other people's opinions do not matter, especially anyone in a position of authority. Breaking the rules and blaming others are signs of this type of low self-esteem. Women who act helpless, are unable to make decisions for themselves, and routinely follow other people's lead might be demonstrating a form of low self-esteem. Underachievement, lack of assertiveness and leaning heavily on others to take the lead are all signs of this type of low self-esteem.

Most of us have very high self-esteem when we are young. However, as we grow up, we are bombarded with negativity. The difference between low self-esteem and high self-esteem is the difference between misery and happiness, between failure and success, between tears and laughter.

Building self-confidence and preparing for success are important in almost every aspect of our lives. Yet so many people struggle to find it. Recovering a sense of self-worth takes more than a change of scenery; it requires a change of perspective. Self-esteem is feeling good about how you see yourself. Self-confidence can be a learned trait, whether you are working on your own confidence or building the confidence of people around you. Confident people inspire confidence in others. From the quietly confident doctor whose advice we rely on, to the charismatic confidence of an inspiring speaker, self-confident people have qualities that everyone admires.

When I was a little girl, I believe I had a certain level of confidence. But there was a part of me that thought I might not be good enough at times. For example, when I was in gym class and two students may have been selected to pick teams, I was always one of the last few they would select. Now don't get me wrong; I was not always the best player, but if I had to run fast, I would always do my best and I always wanted to be on the winning team. It was times like that when my confidence level was low because of not being selected until last. As a child, when you're singled out from others, it can make you feel some type of way. That feeling can also carry over to adulthood when you're singled out in other situations such as promotions or passed over and not invited to an event that one of your so-called friends may have had.

I also remember as a child that I didn't always feel I was beautiful. I always looked at my mother as being a very beautiful woman; she had pretty hair, dressed nice, her skin was so smooth, and she had a certain type of niceness about her. If we went out, my mother would always get compliments about her looks or my dad would get compliments about how beautiful his wife was, but I never heard anyone say I was beautiful. Now, this was during my younger years when I wasn't yet a teenager but still elementary age. I think part of the reason I felt that way is because most of my clothes were hand-me-downs from my brother. My mom didn't always dress me in the fancy girl dresses and outfits, so my appearance affected how I felt. I may have had one or two favorite outfits, but for the most part, I didn't wear any fancy clothes, mainly because I didn't have any. By the time I was twelve going on thirteen, I had my first job and I bought my own clothes. I wouldn't say that I had low self-esteem, but there were times when I may have felt my self-esteem to be lacking.

My parents did pay attention to both my brother and me. They allowed us to learn new things; they smiled and talked to us so there was no negative energy towards us. Overall, I believe as a child, I felt good about myself. I was liked and accepted by my classmates and friends. I would say one thing that boosted my confidence was when Mrs. Barnes, the mother of one of my friends at the time, was a fashion designer and asked me to model some of her designs. Mrs.

Barnes had some beautiful clothes; she was very talented. I was honored to accompany her on some of her viewings modeling her designs. She told me that with some practice, I could be a model. I had the look and I knew how to walk. Next thing you know, I was in my first fashion show. From there, I walked with confidence, with my head up, never looking down.

As a child, my self-confidence developed from my own accomplishments. My self-esteem grew from learning new things, making friends and doing things that I was good at and enjoyed. After the fashion show, I wanted to be a model, so I asked my dad if I could attend Barbizon Modeling school. All of this happened before high school when I was between 11-12 years old. My dad was always supportive, and when he said I could attend the modeling school, I was so happy.

I learned so many things that I believe played a part in building my confidence and self-esteem. Not only did it teach me modeling and the business, but it also taught me how to achieve a confident walk—"the posture of walking"—and health, which included nutrition, fitness, and positive body image. After I attended the school over the summer, I felt as though I could do anything. I entered into some fashion shows and I was also a contestant in a pageant. So, this was the path that I took. I don't even know if they have modeling schools today or if they are as popular as they were back then, but that was one thing that helped me. Another thing that helped me with building self-esteem as a young girl was joining Girl Scouts. The Girl Scouts organization helps young girls build confidence and leadership skills. So, by the time I entered high school, I felt confident.

When I was younger, for some reason, I had this perception of shyness hanging over me. In high school, during the senior superlatives vote, my classmates voted me as "most shy." My brother was outspoken; everyone knew him. He walked down the hall and shook everyone's hands and told jokes in class. He was voted "class clown." I have never considered myself as shy. Most of my friends that have known me for a long time know that I am not shy and would probably laugh when reading this. If I don't know you, I won't talk to you much, but once you are around me and get to know me, you will notice that I am not shy.

Not all shyness is the same. While timidity may be a quirky personality trait, it could also be a sign of social anxiety. Social anxiety is the fear of social situations that involve interaction with other people. You could say social anxiety is the fear and anxiety surrounding being negatively judged and evaluated by other people. It is a pervasive disorder and causes anxiety and fear in most areas of a person's life. I am not saying I have social anxiety, which I don't, but there may be someone reading this that does. The good news is social anxiety is highly treatable with therapy or medication, and you can start by talking to a professional about how you're feeling.

Embracing your awkwardness is the best way to become less awkward. Accept your quirks and all the cool things that make you unique. Maybe it's the gap between your front teeth, your innovative sense of style, or maybe it's the glasses you wear. Accept every part of yourself and surround yourself with people who accept you too!

While you definitely don't have to dress up every day to feel confident, putting a little effort into wearing clothes that make you feel good can help give you that extra boost. Now, as an adult, learn to say NO! It's easy to get taken advantage of when you're under the curse of people-pleasing. Learning how to say no will help build your confidence and keep you from placing your worth in what you can do for others. First, you'll have to accept that it's impossible to make everyone happy and it's not even worth the hassle of trying! It's true that as a black girl, saying no puts us at risk of being cast into the "angry black woman" stereotype or being labeled as difficult and uncooperative. Still, it is important to remember that you always have the right to say no.

What can you do to restore your self-confidence and improve your self-esteem? If you're currently feeling sluggish or just down about your life, it's time for you to get that confidence back up and be the stunning and successful woman you can be. Get a makeover. If you are feeling insignificant, especially about your looks, a great way to get your confidence back up is to get a makeover. Feeling pampered can help you transform your personality into one that shines. Getting rid of the old look that makes you unhappy and replacing it with a new look that makes you smile is enough to give you the confidence you need. Go out and buy some new clothes. Get your makeup done. Get your nails done, or even get a new hairdo. Do anything you want to do to get rid of what makes you unhappy.

I mentioned this earlier, but I'll say it again: *Remove the negativity.* There are some people in your life that will always bring you down, and now is the time to get rid of them. It doesn't matter if it's a friend or family member, but if there is someone out there who is constantly bombarding you with negative energy or information, even if it's not entirely about you, send them to the curb. Along with people you know in real life, it's also a good idea to remove negative people from your online social life too. Unfriend, unfollow or block the negative people out of your life.

Achieve a small goal. We all set large goals for ourselves, and when we don't meet these goals, our confidence tends to suffer. Instead of allowing this to happen, try breaking your large goal down into smaller goals, and then celebrate those achievements.

Exercise, which I will talk about later on in the book. Even if you absolutely hate exercising, you'll be surprised by how a little bit of sweat can go a long way in building your confidence. You'll be able to work off all the stress you've been feeling, and you'll also start to feel better about your body, which can help to boost your confidence levels. Even doing something small, such as taking a walk around the block before you go to work, is enough to ditch the stress and help you to tackle your day better.

Make an achievements list. Sometimes you just need to be reminded of all the good things you're capable of to boost your confidence. Sit down and write a list of everything that you're good at, no matter how big or small it may be. Maybe you're a single mom and have raised your child with no father. Maybe you're good at math and know how to do taxes. Maybe you earned your master's degree. No matter what it is, write it down. Then, look at everything you've done and still do well, and keep that list as a reminder that you are wonderful.

Now, spiritually speaking, the first step is to have faith in God. Trust that no matter the circumstance, your life is in His hands and He will bring you through your situation. The second step on your journey toward greater self-esteem is taking stock of where you are and what you have already achieved, which is similar to what I mentioned earlier. Think about your life and list the things you have done that reflect your determination and strength. The third step is to practice self-esteem affirmations daily. Here are a few to get you started:

> I love and accept myself unconditionally.
>
> I approve of myself and feel great about myself.
>
> I radiate love and respect, and in return, I get love and respect.
>
> I am a well-loved and well-respected person.

> My high self-esteem enables me to respect others and be respected in return.
>
> I am free to make my own choices and decisions.
>
> I am a unique and very special person and worthy of respect from others.

We as women can learn to be more confident and diminish the signs of low self-esteem by taking better care of ourselves. We can take active steps to treat ourselves better and find ways to feel good about our lives. This can include making time for enjoyable activities, putting talents and special abilities to good use, surrounding ourselves with positive people and spending more time with positive friends and family.

What I hope you got out of reading this chapter about self-confidence and self- esteem is to just be you!

"For you formed my inward parts; you covered me in my mother's womb. I will praise you, for I am fearfully and wonderfully made; Marvelous are your works, and that my soul knows very well." **(Psalm 139:13-14)**

Chapter Two *Food for thought* on Courage

Do you have the drive to stand up for yourself? If not, why?

Can you say "NO" when you need to despite others prompting you to always say "YES"? If not, why?

Are you willing to take off your mask of inauthenticity and proudly show your scars of imperfection? If not, why?

CHAPTER 3

Encourage and Believe in Yourself

Life can be very difficult at times. Are you wondering why you aren't getting the compliments and recognition you deserve? Feeling disgruntled because your praiseworthy efforts are not being praised? To make sure you always get the recognition and appreciation you deserve, stop waiting for it to come from someone else. Give it to yourself in a measure equal to what you are entitled to receive.

Being self-encouraged is nearly the same as being self-motivated. Waiting for someone's encouragement is only going to become an exercise and leave you with a sense of frustration. Others are simply too unreliable to give you encouragement when you need it most. Instead of waiting around for that pat on the back, there are several ways to encourage yourself. The first is to be mindful of your small wins and achievements. Make a mental note of them and be sure to recollect them at the end of the day. Secondly, celebrate progress toward your goals. Set yourself up with milestones so that each goal is broken down into manageable chunks that you reward yourself for upon attaining. The third is to bask in the simple pleasure of a good day's work. Know that your efforts will eventually pay off, and be satisfied in the knowledge that hard work is its own reward.

Another way to encourage yourself is to find some peace of mind in the knowledge that you have done right or that you have done enough. This is not to make excuses for yourself; it is to set realistic boundaries so that you are not constantly striving but are pausing to recognize the merits of your achievements and efforts. Also, stay future-focused. Be inspired by your hopes, dreams and plans. Know that the work you are doing is a means to an end. That end will be realized as long as you continue working toward it and focusing on it. Believe that you can; believe that you will.

Giving up is pointless. It serves no purpose other than to prove you are right when you say, "I can't." The simple statement, "I know I can," is encouragement in and of itself. Another way is to surround yourself with positive influences and seek out motivational quotes, positive people or uplifting music. Don't wallow in negative thinking, and don't allow others who are discouraging to steal your joy. Also, if you have confidence and nothing else, at least have confidence enough that you will find a way. If what you are doing doesn't work, be confident that you will find a different way. If you have failed, be confident that you will learn, grow and succeed another time. Confidence is not the ability to do something; confidence is the ability to try again to find a way so that you can eventually succeed.

Take matters into your own hands. Those people who are not encouraging you are not in control of how you feel. The universe that keeps putting obstacles in your way is not in control of how you feel about your day-to-day efforts. You are in control, and seizing that control will be encouraging. Finally, open yourself up to learning and growing because it is hard to find courage in what you already have. It's easier to have courage in what you will become. Encourage yourself by seeking new opportunities for development.

When you encourage yourself, you will feel less deprived of others' encouragement. You will be less reliant on external praise. You won't be as needy, and you will be effective, regardless of what others are or are not saying around you.

The benefit you will gain by encouraging yourself is that you will gain more success in reaching your personal and professional goals. Another benefit is more health and happiness will come naturally when you become your own coach and begin to encourage yourself. Also, you will gain more fulfilling relationships as a natural consequence. When you're a good friend to yourself, it will be much easier for others to be a good friend to you. You will ask less of others, and you will have more to offer.

After you encourage yourself, you may have a desire to encourage or inspire others. How do you encourage others? There have been times where I have encouraged my friends and didn't even realize that I said something that affected them in a way that inspired them to make life changes. When was the last time someone told you, "I'm proud of you," not for what you've done or accomplished, but just for being you? I noticed that I often told someone I was proud of them because of an accomplishment, and I wanted to learn to encourage others just because. Do you know the power of your words? If you are a leader, your words are magnified. Something that seems of no consequence to you can either lift a team member's spirits or crush them. If you are a parent, this power is amplified even more. Whether you are a company leader, a parent, a mentor, or someone that others look up to for any reason, your words hold immense power. That's why it's critical that your words build others up, not tear them down. They must be encouraging.

What is encouragement? Encouragement is telling others that you believe in them before they even start or do something. To encourage others and inspire them to achieve more than they might think is possible, there are a few things you can do, such as showing them you care. When you take the time to learn about others, it shows that you care. This empowers and encourages them. If you are a business leader, the best way to do this is in your one-on-one meetings. Another way is to tell them verbally. Take the time to tell your team, your friends, and your family that you believe in their abilities and that you are confident that they will succeed. You can also tell them in writing. The great thing about encouraging someone in writing is that they can keep the note forever. And if you're not a writer, you can give an inspiring card.

Another way to encourage others is to share your thoughts about them with others. One of the best ways to encourage someone is to tell others how great he or she is. When you speak of your spouse or significant other in public, praise them. When you talk about your children, praise them. At work, when you talk about a team member with a fellow manager, talk him up. Over time, it will create a culture of encouragement. Also, by trusting them with more when you assign responsibility, even if you do not verbalize it, you are saying, "I trust you." Trust conveys belief. Don't just say it if you don't really trust them. When you give someone responsibility, remember you are not only entrusting them with the expectation of success, but you are also allowing them to make mistakes. When you try to "fix" things along the way, it is discouraging and demotivating. Give responsibility, trust the person, and get out of the way.

Finally, you can help them. Not to fix it like I just mentioned, but simply ask how you can help them. It's important for others to know that while you trust them, you are also there to help. At work, this goes beyond just helping with projects or tasks, though. Get involved in their personal development by offering to send them to professional training, seminars, classes, or other learning opportunities. Show them that you care about their self-improvement, not just their work.

The great thing about each of these is that they are effective in any environment. They work in the office, at home, and literally everywhere. When you show that you care, tell others that you believe in them, talk positively about them to others, trust them with important things, and help them succeed, you encourage them to believe in themselves and accomplish more than they thought possible.

I remember one of my good friends living in Virginia at the time wanted to move back to her home state of Arkansas to be closer to her parents. She was a little leery about asking her employer if she would be able to telework from her home state because she was planning to relocate. She knew that if she asked her manager, they would make the assumption that she wanted to leave the job. She actually loved her job and didn't want to leave, but she also wanted to be closer to her aging parents. This friend was also my prayer partner, so one day we prayed about it, and I told her to ask her manager so that she could move forward on her decision about what to do next. Well, things worked out in her favor, and she was able to relocate and still keep her job. Since then her life has changed; she is now married with children and is able to see her parents more frequently with just a two or three-hour drive. About three years after she moved, she told me that I was instrumental in her having the discussion with her employer and moving, and she did not know what her situation would be like today had it not been for my encouragement. It made me feel good to know that I could have a positive impact on someone like that.

People aren't down all the time; they may be experiencing the loss of a family member or someone close to them. Or it could be an illness, loss of a job or failing an exam. I'm going to talk more about experiencing loss later on in the book, but for now, I want you to think about some encouraging words you can say to your family member or friends if they are experiencing loss of a loved one, illness or any of the other situations that may cause someone to feel a little down. What are words of encouragement? Here are some examples of encouraging words:

"Everything you need to accomplish your goals is already in you." Unknown

"The best revenge is massive success." – ***Frank Sinatra***

"When life knocks you down, try to land on your back. Because if you can look up, you can get up." – ***Les Brown***

"Never, never, never give up." – ***Winston Churchill***

"If you don't like something, change it. If you can't change it, change your attitude." – ***Maya Angelou***

"Don't wait around for other people to be happy for you. Any happiness you get you've got to make yourself." – ***Alice Walker***

"Deal with yourself as an individual worthy of respect and make everyone else deal with you the same way." – ***Nikki Giovanni***

"Give light and people will find the way." – ***Ella Baker***

"Surround yourself with only people who are going to lift you higher." – ***Oprah Winfrey***

"You can't make decisions based on fear and the possibility of what might happen." – ***Michelle Obama***

"I am an example of what is possible when girls from the very beginning of their lives are loved and nurtured by people around them. I was surrounded by extraordinary women in my life who taught me about quiet strength and dignity." – ***Michelle Obama***

"Success isn't about how much money you make. It's about the difference you make in people's lives." – ***Michelle Obama***

"The kind of beauty I want most is the hard-to-get kind that comes from within: strength, courage, dignity."- ***Ruby Dee***

"Man, just believe in yourself, be able to dream, and know that there's going to be valleys and peaks. Always stay centered, and know that God is the key, the beginning and end of everything you do." – ***Common***

"You have to stand for what you believe in and sometimes you have to stand alone." – ***Queen Latifah***

"Change will not come if we wait for some other time. We are the ones we've been waiting for. We are the change that we seek." – ***Former President Barack Obama***

What I want you to take away from this chapter of encouragement is to believe in yourself always and don't depend on someone else to lift you up; you have to do it yourself. Believing in yourself will open up endless possibilities in your life. In order to believe in yourself, you first have to believe that what you want is possible. The idea of always having a positive expectation that what you want is going to happen is simply a choice, a discipline of the mind, and the way you think. You have to change your thought process. At times, you may find this difficult to do. The truth is that we've been conditioned throughout our lives to doubt ourselves. We must re-train ourselves to get rid of our fears and self-doubt in order to build self-esteem and self-confidence. Everything you have in your life is a result of your belief in yourself and the belief that it's possible. Believe that you can do it, regardless of what anyone says or where you are in life. Visualize it: think about exactly what your life would look like if you had already achieved your dream.

When you visualize it, you will naturally become more motivated to reach your goals. You'll start to notice you are unexpectedly doing things that move you closer to your ideal life. One way to do this is with a motivational vision board. A vision board is a graphic representation of exactly what you want in life. You look at it every day. Use it to visualize exactly where you want to go. Always act in a way that is consistent with where you want to go. Take action towards your goals. Do not let fear stop you. Nothing happens in life until you take action. If you have faith in your own abilities and work hard, there is nothing you cannot accomplish. If you believe in yourself and have dedication and pride and never quit, you'll be a winner.

Chapter 3 *Food for thought* *Encourage and Believe in Yourself*

What do you do to encourage yourself when going through hard times?

Who do you talk to for encouragement and Inspiration?

CHAPTER 4

Fear Will Fail

Fear is a powerful emotion; it has a very strong effect on your mind and body. Anxiety is a type of fear that usually has to do with the thought of a threat or something going wrong in the future rather than right now.

Fear and anxiety can last for a short time and then pass. I believe both fear and anxiety have blocked my blessings. There have been things that I either wanted to do or didn't try hard enough to do because I allowed fear to control me. What I have learned is that we should not try to get over fear, but we should go through it instead. Let yourself be afraid, and then just do it! You will be afraid for a moment, but then it will pass. Understand fear and embrace it. Fear exists to keep us safe. It is not inherently bad or good, but it is a tool we can use to make better decisions. Fear isn't designed to keep us inactive, but to help us act in ways that generate the results we need and want. Embrace fear as instruction and let it inform your actions but not control them.

One of my fears is speaking in public. Either I would get nervous and start sweating, or I would find a way to get out of the situation. In 2014, one of my best friends, Va'Nechia, passed away after battling cancer. Her family asked me to speak at the funeral about friendship, and I said yes. I was grieving, but I didn't want to let her family down, plus I knew my friend would be happy that I spoke at her funeral. I was in a state of fear because I had to speak in front of a large group of people in a church.

Va'Nechia's funeral was packed; she was a teacher and active in her community, so a lot of people came to her funeral and it was standing room only. Before the funeral, I prepared talking points and wrote them down on a notecard. When the time came for me to speak, I walked up to the pulpit and looked out and saw all of those people, then I looked over at my friend's mom, and I smiled. I looked at my note cards and started to speak; I started off talking about how Va'Nechia and I met and became friends then I started telling stories and people laughed. I started to get into it and the next thing I knew, I wasn't afraid anymore. I went through it and I faced that fear. After it was over, I went to my seat and cried, not in the sense of relief from speaking, but because I was going to miss my best friend.

There have been other situations where speaking in public brought out the fear in me, including instances where I have had to give a presentation at work in front of a group of men and women. My career has been in Information Technology (IT) for over twenty years. It has been tough at times because it is a male-dominated field for the most part, and I'm always in a situation where I have to prove myself. For some reason, some men believe women shouldn't be in this field and that they don't know enough. So anytime I had to do a presentation I would get a sense of fear that I would say the wrong thing, and I was even a little intimidated by the audience. So, what I did was invest in myself and take a public speaking class. It helped me to overcome that fear so that anytime I am speaking, I am prepared, and depending on the audience, I am speaking from the heart. Now, don't get me wrong, I still get nervous, but I get through it and let it flow.

There are different types of fear, but no matter what type of fear you have, you can get through it. The fear of rejection is a very common human emotion. Sometimes we don't want to admit that we have a fear of being rejected. When you think you have overcome the fear of rejection, you may realize that there are still some deeper issues. If you embrace the fear, you will feel more comfortable with yourself and the others around you when your subtle subconscious waves make you doubt what you say, do, or don't say or do because you fear the criticism and judgments of others. When you think you're being criticized, you feel rejected and unaccepted. In some situations, that may lead to embarrassment and trigger fear. Some of us fear saying or doing something that others, especially our own parents, may judge. I never wanted to disappoint my parents, so I always did what I was told. If I did something that I felt my parents wouldn't like, I would keep it to myself.

Another situation where we fear rejection is when we meet a potential mate and start to doubt ourselves because we want the person to like us. Dealing with romantic rejection is notoriously tough. Whether you struggle with how to deal with rejection from a man, the feelings of pain and shame are the same. You may feel undesirable, uninteresting and pessimistic about the prospect of finding love. Note to yourself, if this person doesn't like you, you are not rejected! If the person doesn't like you, then they're probably not for you; he or she is not your match.

Fear of rejection can come in different forms; it could be the fear of being accepted on a team. I attended a historically black college for my first two years of college, and at the time, the school had one of the best cheerleading teams in the Central Intercollegiate Athletic Association (CIAA) conference. They were not just cheerleaders, but they were also athletic, very fit, and they were very good and well-known. I wanted to try-out, so I attended an information session, but when it came time for try-outs, I did not show up. I feared that I would not be able to do the routines and that I would be rejected.

Feeling rejected hurts. It undermines your confidence and makes you doubt your worth. And whether you've experienced it a lot, or it has happened only once or twice in your life, it can easily lead to anxiety about future rejection. At work, you might feel rejected for professional or social reasons. Perhaps you feel you're often passed over promotion or not asked to take on exciting new responsibilities. Alternatively, maybe you struggle to fit in with your colleagues and feel they don't like you or don't invite you to spend time with them.

While working in the field of Information Technology, the majority of the time, I have been the only female and African American on the team. I often felt the fear of rejection concerning work assignments and even socially when the guys would go out for lunch but wouldn't invite me. When you feel rejected, you think about how other people see you, and you assume they see you negatively. Rejection makes you believe you can't really achieve your dreams. Anytime you feel rejected, you think about how you must not seem interesting or worthwhile to other people. Rejection leaves you thinking that you aren't intelligent, talented or capable. Being rejected leads you to imagine how disappointing you are to people you care about. You work hard to make people have low expectations of you so that they won't expect you to succeed. When you're going to do something that might lead to rejection, physical symptoms of anxiety such as stomach pains and tension headaches sometimes stop you from doing that thing. If you think you will end up feeling rejected, you find other tasks to do that will help you avoid the risk. You find excuses to remove yourself from circumstances where you might feel rejected, telling yourself you have no other choice.

The only way to deal with fear is to address it head-on. Dealing with it directly helps me. For some, it may be a natural tendency to deny that you have a problem caused by fear of some kind. You become afraid of confronting it. In turn, it becomes a major source of stress and unhappiness, and it may cause unnecessary illness.

Whatever your fear is, be willing to deal with the situation or person directly. Name the fear. Sometimes, merely stating what your fear is will give you the strength to deal with it. Say your fear out loud, write it down, or focus your mind on it. When you try to ignore your fear, it grows. When you face it, it shrinks.

When you force yourself to face any fear-inducing situation in your life, your self-esteem goes up, your self-respect increases and your sense of personal pride grows.

You eventually reach the point in life where you are not afraid of anything.

Another way to overcome your fear is to visualize yourself performing with confidence and competence in an area where you are fearful. Your visual image will eventually be accepted by your subconscious mind as instructions for your performance.

Your self-image, the way you see yourself and think about yourself, is eventually altered by feeding your mind these positive mental pictures of yourself performing at your best. It's one of those situations where you see yourself doing what you are afraid of, and you overcome it.

I believe it is important that you confront your fears as soon as you possibly can. Your ability to confront and deal with your feelings and act in spite of your fears is the key to happiness and success.

One of the best exercises you can practice is to identify a person or situation in your life of which you are afraid and resolve to deal with that situation immediately.

Do not allow it to make you unhappy for another minute. Resolve to confront the situation or person and put the fear behind you.

One of the greatest breakthroughs you can have is through developing the courage you desire by disciplining yourself repeatedly to do the thing you fear until that fear eventually disappears, and it will.

Whatever it is that scares you, find ways to help you cope with your day-to-day fears and anxieties such as taking a time out. It's impossible to think clearly when your mind is overcome with fear or anxiety. The first thing to do is take time out so you can physically calm down. Distract yourself from the worry for fifteen minutes by going for a walk, getting some fresh air or even taking a bath. Another way to calm down is to take a deep breath or try a breathing technique by placing the palm of your hand on your stomach and breathing slowly and deeply.

You can try imagining the worst thing that can happen, and the fear will run away the more you chase it. Sharing fears takes away a lot of their scariness. Whatever you're afraid of, is it something you have to do alone? Can you find a mentor or support group to help you through it? If you cannot talk to a partner, friend or family member, seek a counselor or therapist.

Educate yourself. We are afraid of nothing so much as the unknown. If your fear is based on a lack of information, then get the information or knowledge you need to examine the situation based on facts rather than speculation.

Follow others; find a recipe. Are you doing something that has never been done, or can you follow in the footsteps of someone else who has accomplished it before? Is there a formula for success? Has someone written a book on the topic, or can you tweak a formula from another field to meet your needs?

Now, if you feel a sense of anxiety, you may need to go back to the basics—the simple, everyday things like a good night's sleep, a wholesome meal and a walk are often the best cures for anxiety.

Once you have done what was needed and you're feeling better, give yourself a treat. When you have made that call you have been dreading and faced the fear head-on, reinforce your success by treating yourself to a massage, a walk, a meal out, a movie, or whatever little gift makes you happy.

Finally, there are different types of fears and phobias. Don't allow fear to hold you back from success. You can be your worst enemy, so regardless of your occupation, understand that taking risks and massive action is a vital part of getting from where you are to where you want to go. And that goes for in life and business. Often when these risks are met with fear, it can cause people to question their ambitions and prevent them from taking action.

One thing I would like you to understand is that fear is absolutely normal. The key is not to let fear hold you back and prevent you from taking action and going after what you want in life. Rewiring your brain is one of the surest ways to overcome your fears and develop the courage that is needed to get to where you want to go. Develop mantras and affirmations that build you up and increase your self-confidence. Read uplifting books to help interrupt the negative inner thoughts that go on in your mind. Have a well thought out plan. We begin to worry and over-analyze situations when we don't have detailed and well thought out plans for our life. Set extremely clear goals with a detailed plan on how to achieve those goals. After you have a well-detailed plan, take action. Taking action towards meaningful goals helps to relieve stress and gives you a huge sense of enjoyment. Fear creeps in and paralyzes us when we don't take the time to plan our lives.

Living in our comfort zone is not the best way to live. Not doing the things that frighten you will increase the likelihood that your fears will become bigger and take over your life. It can even be something small that you choose to do, but do something daily that scares you. Step out of your comfort zone and work on becoming comfortable with the uncomfortable. When you form the habit of doing something daily that scares you, your courage grows little by little. Soon enough, the barriers that were once holding you back vanish, and your potential maximizes tremendously.

Making the bold decision not to let fear hold you back anymore is one of the best decisions you can make to ensure future success. It's not something that happens overnight, but taking intentional action and running towards your fears daily will give you a promising result in the long run.

Everything that you want in life is past your comfort zone. Don't let fear be the reason you live a half-lived life. Live your best life!

Chapter 4 *Food for thought* on *Fear will Fail*

What are some of your biggest, most obvious fears?

Is there something in your life that you really want to do, or a certain passion or dream you have, but aren't doing because you're scared? If so, what can you do about it now to change the situation?

CHAPTER 5

Being Brave

I wrote an article about bravery in the past, and I want to share that with you because often we lack the courage to do something.

Brave means listening to the still, small voice inside and DOING AS IT SAYS, regardless of what the rest of the world is saying.

Courage is "having strength in the face of pain or grief." Courage is the ability to act on one's beliefs despite danger or disapproval. Courage is also called daring, audacity, boldness, grit, true grit, hardihood, heroism, and gallantry, among other things.

Below are a few scriptures that will help you to be brave, strong and of courage:

"Wait on the LORD; be of good courage, And He shall strengthen your heart; Wait, I say, on the LORD!" ***(Psalm 27:14)***

Watch, stand fast in the faith, be brave, be strong. Let all that you do be done with love."
(1 Corinthians 16:13-14)

"Be strong and of good courage, do not fear nor be afraid of them; for the Lord your God, He is the One who goes with you. He will not leave you nor forsake you." ***(Deuteronomy 31:6)***

"Be strong and of good courage, for to this people you shall divide as an inheritance the land which I swore to their fathers to give them." ***(Joshua 1:6)***

"For God has not given us a spirit of fear, but of power and of love and of a sound mind."
(2 Timothy 1:7)

"I can do all things through Christ[a] who strengthens me."
(Philippians 4:1)

"Blessed be the Lord my Rock, who trains my hands for war, and my fingers for battle." ***(Psalm 144:1)***

"The Lord will fight for you, and you shall hold your peace." ***(Exodus 14:14)***

"Be still and know that I am God; I will be exalted among the nations; I will be exalted in the earth!" ***(Psalm 46:10)***

"The Lord is my helper; I will not fear. What can man do to me? ***(Hebrews 13:6)***

"Finally, my brethren, be strong in the Lord and in the power of His might." ***(Ephesians 6:10)***

"Have I not commanded you? Be strong and of good courage; do not be afraid, nor be dismayed, for the Lord your God is with you wherever you go." ***(Joshua 1:9)***

"You are of God, little children, and have overcome them, because He who is in you is greater than he who is in the world."
(1 John 4:4)

"And He said to me, "My grace is sufficient for you, for My strength is made perfect in weakness." Therefore, most gladly I will rather boast in my infirmities, that the power of Christ may rest upon me."
(2 Corinthians 12:9)

Brave means feeling afraid and doing it anyway. Brave means saying NO when those around you want you to say yes. Brave means taking a leap of faith, even when you're not sure how things will turn out. Brave means getting up and walking out into the sunshine even when the circumstances of your life make you want to stay in the dark. Brave is shouting out loud, and brave is also staying quiet. Brave is when you stay true to your heart. Your brave is different from my brave. When you find the place inside you where your truest desires meet your deepest fears, that's where you'll find your brave.

Be Brave, Be Bold, Be Strong.

Chapter Five *Food for thought* on *Being Brave*

How can you be courageous and brave?

How do you show bravery?

CHAPTER 6

Stress is Stalking You

Do you often feel like you have a monkey on your back? You have no control; people are demanding top performance from you at work, and personal circumstances are piling up. What is stress? Stress is your body's way of responding to any kind of demand or threat. Stress can be good or bad. Good stress may help you stay focused, energetic, and alert. Stress can help you rise to meet challenges. It's what keeps us on our toes at work; it sharpens our concentration.

Good stress motivates you. It can propel you forward and help you achieve more goals, ultimately leading to more happiness, success, or fulfillment. Good stress may occur during events and moments in an individual's life when a certain level of motivation is needed to overcome a potentially difficult obstacle. Good stress is associated with the excitement of identifying and overcoming obstacles. Good stress is temporary, and an example could be running a race or preparing for an exam. After the event is over, that good stress goes away.

Bad stress, if not relieved, can be detrimental to your health. Bad stress is also known as distress, which manifests itself as chronic or ongoing stress that begins to hinder your everyday life and stops you from completing tasks.

How stressed are you? Do you actually know how stressed you are? You might be overly stressed without even knowing it. Maybe you have certain physical symptoms and blame it on an illness or other condition. But the truth is, stress itself can cause problems in your organs, tissues, and just about every system in your body. Depending on how you handle stress, you might have symptoms that affect everything from your hormones to your heart, and more. Pain or tension in your head, chest, stomach, or muscles are indications of stress. Your muscles tend to tense up when you're stressed, and over time, this can cause headaches and migraines. You can develop digestive problems, which can include diarrhea, constipation, nausea and vomiting. Stress can affect how quickly food moves through your system and the way your intestines absorb nutrients. I did not know this at first, but I had digestive problems and didn't know that a culprit was stress.

Stress can cause changes to your sex drive, problems with irregular or painful periods in women, or impotence and problems with sperm production in men. Whether you're a man or a woman, you might also feel reduced sexual desire when you're under too much stress. If you notice changes to your heart rate and blood pressure, that can be a sign. When you're overwhelmed with stress, your body sets off triggers in your adrenal glands to release the hormones cortisol and adrenaline. These hormones can make your heart beat faster and your blood pressure rise. This usually happens when there's a momentary stressor, and the effects pass once it's over. For example, you might find your heart racing if you're late for a meeting, but then it calms down once you arrive. However, over time, too many episodes of acute stress can cause inflammation in your arteries, which could be a contributing factor to heart attacks.

My father had a few heart attacks, and I suspected that stress was one of the reasons. He worked a lot of hours, lacked sleep, and he also didn't have the best diet. As I have grown into an adult, observing some of the things that happened to my dad makes me think twice about doing it myself so that I can possibly avoid what he has experienced.

Stress can also affect how you think and feel, making it tough to get through your normal responsibilities and make rational decisions. In some cases, this kind of stress can impact behavior in other ways, and some people turn to drugs, alcohol, tobacco, or other harmful substances to cope with their feelings. Excessive stress may also affect your appetite, causing you to eat more or less than usual, and it may affect or eliminate your motivation to exercise and stay fit. Additionally, the feelings you get when you're stressed may make you feel like withdrawing from friends and family and isolating yourself. Unfortunately, I have experienced these symptoms and allowed them to get the best of me. Overeating and withdrawing from friends and family were some of the things that I did in response to stress.

Stress and the Working Woman

Everyone in today's supercharged workplace experiences stress. Yet research shows that executive and professional women consistently experience more stress, anxiety, and psychological distress than men. There are, undoubtedly, a variety of reasons for this, which include women having more domestic responsibilities, having been socialized to say "yes" to all requests, and receiving lower pay for similar work. Being a woman, I know that women can suffer considerably higher levels of work-related stress, anxiety and depression, probably more than men, with workplace sexism and family responsibilities providing additional career pressures.

Why are women always asked to help with group projects at work, such as planning parties and activities of that nature? That can be fulfilling, but it can also be stressful. This pressure reaches a peak for women aged thirty-five to forty-four, when many of them are juggling family responsibilities, such as caring for children and elderly parents. Women face additional workplace pressures, such as having to prove they are as good as men, not being valued or promoted, receiving unequal pay, and being expected to look the part. Research shows that female managers in male-dominated fields sometimes find the strain intolerable, and their stress levels are also rising because families are more reliant on their income. As for me, being a single woman, I rely one hundred percent on my income; there is no husband, and I am the only breadwinner.

I have worked in a male-dominated field all my life, in the industry of Information Technology, and I can definitely say that I have been unhappy about job security, lack of potential for career progression, and receiving lower pay than my male colleagues. I recall not long after graduating from college, I took a job at a Fortune 500 company as a help desk analyst. During that time, I started out making fifty thousand dollars a year, and I thought I was doing great until I overheard a few of my white male counterparts discussing their starting salaries of sixty thousand dollars a year. They were straight out of college as well, but the thing is, I had experience because I worked at a help desk before, but these guys were fresh out of college with no experience, white, and one of them knew a top executive at the company. For the four years I worked at that company, I tried to get increases in pay, but it didn't come easy. And by the time l left and moved on, I was just beginning to get the pay the white men were making when I started, which means they were making much more by that time.

There have been instances where my position was threatened due to not having a particular IT certification. That caused me so much stress that my doctor told me that I should consider another line of work because the stress was not good for my health. Women face so much stress for various reasons in the workplace that the solution shouldn't always be leaving the job. It's not that easy to just up and quit, especially if you are the only breadwinner in the family.

When I first moved to the Washington D.C. area, I had a job with an organization in which the Director touched me inappropriately. When the incident occurred, I couldn't believe that it happened. My manager was a witness and allowed it to happen and did nothing. So, as I walked out of the office, I thought to myself, this isn't right, and I'm going to say something. So I went back into the office, called him out on it, and told him that I didn't appreciate him touching me in that way. I did this with my manager and another male present in the office and they didn't do anything. The director then apologized, but I can tell you this, both he and my manager created a hostile work environment for me.

I was stressed. I had just moved from New Jersey to Washington, D.C., and in less than a year on the job, I was experiencing sexual harassment and a hostile work environment. The hostility included my manager paging me for no reason. During that time, we didn't have cell phones; we had pagers, and when I would go to lunch, he would page me for no reason. When I would return to the office, he would question where I was and why I didn't respond to his page right away.

I filed a complaint with the organization's civil rights office, but they told me that I didn't have enough information to launch an investigation. I didn't know what to do, but I knew that I couldn't stay in that environment, so I eventually found another job and left. But these are the types of stressful situations that women have to deal with. Not to mention discrimination for being a black woman. I work in a male-dominated field, and the majority of the time, I am the only female sitting at the table and sometimes the only African American in the room. I can honestly say I have had my share of stress in the workplace, and it has affected my health. I have gained weight and experienced tension headaches, depression and high blood pressure.

How did you overcome workplace stress? Well, you can do a few things. You can eliminate what you can; you don't have to be the office party planner. When you go to work, do your job, but you don't have to plan the parties and office activities if you have a ton of work on your desk to do. For me, I ended up leaving that job and finding another. To maintain a reasonable level of daily stress, we as women need to get used to the idea of setting priorities and saying no.

Alter your perspective. Much of our experience with stress can be eliminated with a change in the way we look at things. Alter the way you conceptualize the events you find stressful by viewing them as "challenges" instead of "threats," or "opportunities" instead of "crises." For example, if you're asked to plan a retirement party, look at it as an opportunity to collaborate with others and possibly meet employees from other departments. You may come into contact with people that you didn't know before, and you never know who is watching your work.
When you don't perceive a situation as a threat, your body's stress response is deactivated more quickly, or it doesn't get triggered in the first place. Another way to help with workplace stress is to have some quick stress relievers, such as practicing meditation and praying or exercising daily. Journaling may also have some benefits. Journal your feelings in the morning or night and just get it all out on paper.

There are several ways to manage your stress. You can also create a personal wellness plan with goals. You can include a review of life areas and examine the areas for potential change. Identify goals, be aware of what needs to be done, and set goals. Be specific and know what you want to accomplish. Be realistic and set smaller goals that are achievable. Identify resources and use helpful resources to reduce potential problems. Set time limits, but don't stress yourself out. Just consider reasonable, specific time limits. Evaluate your progress and make changes as needed.

I find creating a plan and writing it down to be very helpful, that way I'm not overloading my mind with all of the things that I need to do. We, as women, will continue to experience stress in our lives. I find that self-care helps me manage stress, and it's empowering me to make healthy life changes. Here are some of the self-care activities that I like to do: take a hot shower or warm bubble bath, listen to running water, and when the weather is nice, I love to sit outdoors and soak in the fresh air. One of my favorite things to do is get a massage and burn a scented candle while listening to music.

A great way to take care of yourself when you're coping with stress is to engage in a pleasurable activity. I love to take pictures, so I go on a photo walk. I will take myself out to eat and a movie. The solo trip gives me peace of mind; it is time that I don't have to be concerned about anyone or anything.

I hope if you are stressed and you are reading this, you now know the symptoms and seek help. I would only go to my doctor when it was time for my annual physical, so of course, I would say what my symptoms were, but you really should go to the doctor when the symptoms appear, especially when it relates to the heart.

Chapter Six *Food for thought* on *Stress is Stalking You*

Have you been under stress recently?

____

____

____

____

How is stress affecting you?

____

____

____

____

____

____

How can you eliminate the stress in your life? Be honest!

____

____

____

____

____

____

CHAPTER 7

Invest in Yourself

Ever since I can remember, I have always done something to improve or make myself better, whether it is work-related or personal. When I was in middle school, I was interested in modeling, so I convinced my parents to send me to modeling school. After I graduated from high school, I went to college because I thought by doing that, I would get a good job. Throughout my career, I have always invested in myself. When you are working different jobs, you can't always depend on people to show you what to do. When I chose a career in Information Technology, I knew there would be things I would have to learn on my own. Throughout my career, I have always tried to stay abreast of and keep up with new technologies. To become more skilled, I took additional classes in areas of interest such as web design, network and desktop support and cybersecurity; I even enrolled in a master's program and received a Master of Science degree in Management Information Systems. I did all of this so I could become a better me.

If you don't know where to start or what to do to invest in yourself, the first thing you can do is determine what you like to do or what you are passionate about. If you believe that you need to get better at it, then that is what you will need to do. If you want to be a photographer and take better photos, then take a class; learn the ins and outs of photography from lighting to knowing how to use your camera. If you want to be a hairstylist, then you have to go to cosmetology school; if you want to be the best Executive chef on your side of town, then you have to go to culinary school and learn the different flavors and spices for cooking.

Go for your dreams; live your dreams! Refuse to settle for doing one thing, and don't allow obstacles to get in your way. There may be challenges. You may not be able to afford to take a class, but you can find a way to teach yourself how to do something. There are many free "how-to" videos on YouTube that will help you along the way. Investing in yourself is one of the best things that you can do for yourself.

There are different areas in your life to invest in, or should I say, upgrade yourself. You can improve your quality of life in areas such as physical health, intelligence, character, relationships, finances, emotional health, and career. Good physical health has benefits, from decreasing stress to increasing your energy and your lifespan.

Taking time to improve your skills and what you can offer to the world can be one of the most profitable decisions you'll ever make. Not only does it improve your career options, but it also increases your overall life satisfaction. It gives you a sense of satisfaction and fulfillment. When you get to see the results of your hard work, you feel accomplished. By making small, positive changes that help you invest in yourself, you will be improving your future in the long run. You will be setting yourself up to be able to look back and be thankful for the small investments that you made. Regardless of what your current situation is, it has been largely impacted by the decisions you have made in the past. As a result, you become happier in everything you do. Also, feeling a sense of satisfaction will inspire you to continue investing in yourself so you can reach your potential.

Investing in yourself keeps you motivated. Investing in yourself inspires you to try new things and make your dreams come true. Little by little, as you see the positive differences you are making in your own life, you will want to push even further to continue on your positive path of growth. Investing in yourself motivates you to move forward and helps you break free and get out of your comfort zone. The farther outside of your comfort zone you get, the more you will realize your potential. As you continue to take risks and venture into unknown areas, you will reap more rewards. You will learn new things and learn not to be complacent and satisfied with mediocrity.

Back in 2012, I discovered that I had a gift for creative writing. I love to write stories or inspirational articles that lift people up, especially women. So, I started writing articles and newsletters for my church, and I wanted to do more to inspire women. I decided to write a book, but I wasn't sure where to start until I met my now mentor, Tressa Azarel Smallwood, who was teaching a "Write and Publish Like a Pro" class. I signed up for the course and learned how to write a book in twenty-one days and how to publish and market the book. The course pretty much covered all the ins and outs of writing a book and the business behind the process. You see, I invested in myself, and I felt good about the results and the outcome. That connection with Tressa also opened up the opportunity for me to learn how to write for television and film. This is something I am very excited about, and it has motivated me to do so much more in the TV and film industry. If I didn't take the first step in writing that article or newsletter, it would not have led me to write a book and much more.

Investing in yourself is a way to secure your future. Some jobs don't last long, and most jobs certainly don't last a lifetime. No matter how great you are at your job, how perfect your skills are, or how large your network is, your job is not secured for the rest of your life. The world is always progressing, and with technological advances, certain jobs have become obsolete. However, this also means that new jobs have become available. You always need to be ready, so never stop learning.

There is no guarantee of long-term employment. One day, as time passes and you get a little older, you'll realize that you should have learned more things when you were young and kept up with the changing times. That way, you could have prepared for a more stable future. You don't want to stop and realize one day that you have to catch up on a lot of knowledge to get with the times. You want to remain on top of things.

Investing in yourself gives you the confidence to interact with other people. Investing in your knowledge can take several forms, and learning new things is one way to invest in yourself. When you are knowledgeable about certain areas of specialization, you become confident enough to speak out. Read books, articles, and reports on anything that has to do with what you're interested in. Stay on top of the latest trends so you can always be prepared to talk about what is going on in the world with other people.

When you invest in yourself, you'll learn to take care of yourself and love yourself a little more. This usually starts with self-assessment. To be effective, a self-assessment has to take your values, interests, natural talents, and personality type into account. These characteristics embody who you are, so leaving any of them out won't give you an accurate assessment of yourself. Doing this will help you realize that there are more things that you can do, and unlocking them will help you unleash your potential. It is easier now more than ever before to expand your skillset because of the resources available both online and in communities. Outlining your strengths and weaknesses can help you identify the areas in your life where you can make extra investments to build on your existing strengths.

There are so many ways to invest in yourself. You can start by planning your days and weeks. Time is very valuable, so make sure you manage yours well. If necessary, start a time diary in which you write down how you spend your time. For just one day, write down everything that you want to accomplish, and then keep a record of everything that you actually do. At the end of the day, see how your goals match up with what you actually did. You can start journaling. Studies show that journal writing reduces the risks of stress, depression, and anxiety. It gives you time to reflect on your life and what you are grateful for, and it also provides you with a platform to record your innermost thoughts.

While investing in yourself, you will need to set your long-term and short-term goals. This can be divided into personal goals, career goals, business goals, and others you may think of. Setting a goal provides a direction, a clear focus, and a sense of purpose and motivation. If you don't take the necessary time to set goals for yourself, you will end up spinning your wheels, not knowing where you're going, and wasting precious time. While setting goals, be sure to set specific timeframes so you can keep yourself accountable and measure your progress. Make sure that your goals are SMART goals, meaning they are specific, measurable, attainable, relevant, and time-sensitive.

Investing in yourself can also mean going to places you have never been to before. Traveling exposes you to various different cultures. Sometimes it's not enough just to see the different places in your books; you need to go out there and experience them. Traveling is the perfect way to expose yourself to the vast diversity that exists in our world. From food to traditional ceremonies and holidays, it's amazing to see the unique ways various ethnic groups celebrate life and the customs that determine everyday living. I absolutely love to travel! I make it a priority to go someplace I haven't been each year. I love the experience of seeing different cultures and different countries.

Spend on experiences rather than material things. The problem with spending your money on things such as designer bags and clothes is that the happiness you get from them quickly fades. This is because you quickly get used to having new possessions, and you will continue to raise the bar for even better possessions. On the contrary, every experience you have is new and different from the last and will change who you are, even if just a little. Instead of spending money on things that wear out, it's better to invest in creating memories with yourself and your loved ones. This year I attended The American Black Film Festival (ABFF) for the first time, and I learned so much about the television and film industry. It was definitely an investment for me, being exposed to some of America's top black actors, directors, producers, and writers. I could have spent that money on clothing or shoes, something that doesn't bring value, but because I have an interest in something specific, I decided to invest in myself by attending that festival which educated me about the industry.

Put some effort into how you look. Invest in your appearance, but don't break the bank trying to do that. While character is more important than appearances, it doesn't hurt to look your best always. The better you feel about your appearance, the more confidence you will exude. This means making sure that your clothes are up-to-date and free from holes or tears, and that they are tailored to fit you well.

Hone your set of skills. The skills you have right now are already established. Now you need to develop those skills and improve them until you become an expert. Discovering your skills will help you build your working life around your strengths. As I mentioned earlier, I have been working in the area of Information Technology for pretty much my entire career. Skills are very important in this field, and you need to know how to do something or understand how a certain device or network works. All of this takes skills, and I spent a lot of time learning these skills.

So, take a look at the themes that often come up in your life, or the ways you choose to spend your downtime. What do people come to you for advice about? Reflecting on these things will help you determine and isolate your strengths. If you don't have a skill, guess what? Learn a new skill.

The secret to success in anything you do in life is this: never stop learning. Whether you've earned an advanced degree or you're just starting out in a new career, it's always important to continue to learn new skills. It's especially important to learn new skills that are transferable from one career to another. This ensures that you will remain marketable in an increasingly competitive economy.

I can't express this enough, but take new courses or apply for online classes. Increase your knowledge of things that interest you. If you want to expand your skillset but you're not sure where to start, write down a list of things you are passionate about and narrow down the things that you want to learn how to do. Attend seminars, workshops, and other learning events.

Expand your knowledge by joining forums, seminars, and workshops. This helps you interact with other people who have the same interests as you. Read both educational and recreational books. Reading has a lot of benefits; aside from stimulating your brain, it also helps improve your relaxation response and regulates your heart rate. Books and audiobooks are both great resources for helping you build your knowledge and expertise in any subject. Also, read self-help and self-care blogs and websites. Instead of spending your online time browsing through your Facebook or Instagram feeds, wouldn't it be a better use of your time to read self-care websites? Now, don't get me wrong, because not everything on social media is necessarily a waste of your time. Reading significant material, whether it comes from a social media site or from a reputable source, can be an investment in your life. Reading first-hand accounts of other people's perspectives can be enlightening and truly helpful on your journey to your better self.

Investing in yourself can also mean you need to be a part of an organization. Being in a group gives you a sense of belonging. No matter what organization you're a part of, show up ready to participate, and be active in the mission or common goal. When you are a part of something significant, it gives you a feeling of satisfaction and fulfillment.

Keep your mind, body, and soul healthy. Taking care of yourself and living a healthy lifestyle is one way to invest in yourself. Without a healthy body, you won't be able to accomplish your goals. Eat right every day by fueling your body with essential nutrients. I'm going to talk more about your body later in Chapter 9, "The Temple."

Make time for your friends and family. More than money and other material things, you need to invest time in your loved ones. These are going to be the people who are there for you at the end of the day if your business venture fails or you have a personal emergency. Don't put your work ahead of your family when it comes to your priorities. Get rid of toxic people. You can't be with someone who keeps pulling you down. Help yourself stay positive by choosing your friends wisely. More importantly, stay with those who share your values and principles and who want to be successful and happy, too.

Handle your finances well. One way to do this is by setting up a financial planner. Budget your income and expenses. What I do is set a monthly savings goal. The key is to live within your means. Don't spend more money than you make, and don't spend money that you don't have. Pay yourself first, meaning put money into a savings account whenever you get paid before spending it on other things. Pay your debts and start saving. You can pay your debts first before starting to save, or you can do it the other way around. In reality, it really depends on what works best for you. But either way, if you have debt, it is dragging you down. Until you're free from your debt, your money does not truly belong to you.

Investing in yourself can mean expanding your network. Successful people didn't stay in their rooms waiting for luck to find them. They chased after their dreams by introducing their creations to different successful people who have come before them. The important thing to remember about expanding your network is that you never know where you might meet that one person who can make a huge difference in your world. You may make a network connection one day and not think much of it, but months later, you reach back out to that person because you remember something they said that seemed small at the time, but is now hugely relevant to your life. You can make connections in places that you least expect, so never let your guard down.

Venture into small business and become an entrepreneur. As an addition to your regular job, you might want to start a small business venture to earn some extra income. With an ever-changing economy, it is ideal to have multiple streams of income. You can no longer rely on one job or one source of income to pay your bills. It might help if you side hustle a job you are really passionate about. That way, you won't have to feel the pressure of working more hours during the week because you will already be doing what you love anyway. Having more control over your money will reduce your risk of losing your single revenue source.

Find an expert mentor. Depending on your needs, look for someone who can inspire you and guide you through your journey to success. This can be a business coach or a personal mentor. Learn from their stories and find strength from their experiences. A coach can help you put all of your strategies into action and be a partner in your success. It is their job to help you create and implement your plan for success so you can become your best self.

Keep track of your results. Monitor your investments by checking your progress now and then. Seeing that you have accomplished something motivates you to keep on moving forward.

Choose to be happier. Invest in your happiness by staying positive in whatever you do. Be grateful for what you have and what you still have to achieve. Remember that happiness is a choice. You can always look at the glass as being half full. Happy people never feel held hostage by their circumstances. They find reasons to be grateful, and they find solutions to the obstacles they are facing. Investing in yourself to change your life's potential can be a lot of work. It's not something you can accomplish overnight. But then again, it is worth the effort. I hope reading this has opened your eyes to investing in yourself. It is an important part of living a successful life. I hope you can successfully reach your potential. Investing in yourself is a powerful message to everyone that you can achieve your goals.

Chapter Seven *Food for thought* on *Invest in Yourself*

What are your life goals? What steps can you take to accomplish them?

What type of company do you keep? Do you surround yourself with like-minded people ?

CHAPTER 8

Grief is a Journey

The worst thing that could happen is to get a phone call that someone you love has passed away. In March 2009, my dad passed away from complications of colon cancer.

Whatever you love, whether it's a person or pet, you will one day lose someone you love. When you lose what you love, whether by separation or death, you will grieve that loss. Everyone grieves each individual loss differently. When my father died, I felt a lot of different emotions. I was sad and I felt all alone. Sadness, yearning and loneliness are often part of grieving. We may experience guilt or anger, or even relief or fear.

It is natural to feel sadness. The death of a parent is unlike that of a child or spouse. Neither is easier or harder, just different. Each of us responds to death differently. We will not all respond to grief in the same way because we are all different and unique.

Do you actually get over it? How do you move on with life without them? Getting over the loss of a loved one can be one of the hardest challenges that we may face in our lifetime. Although loss is understood as a natural part of life, we can be overcome by shock, confusion, and prolonged periods of sadness and depression. The truth is everyone reacts to death differently; it may take months or even years to come to terms with a loss. There is no normal time period for someone to grieve, and some of us may even be in denial during grief.

Mourning the loss of a relative or close friend takes time. While I was grieving the loss of my father, I found myself crying throughout the day. There would be some days where I would just start crying. I also found Father's Day to be hard to get through. I knew I had to move on with my life. My father would not want me to sit around crying and moping around the house. I went through a period of depression, and I also questioned why God had to take my father; asking why he couldn't be healed from cancer. After seeking some counsel from my church, I came to grips with the fact that it was God's will, and I eventually started feeling better after taking it one day at a time.

There were a few things that helped me get through the grief. One thing I learned was that it helps to talk about the death of a loved one with friends and family to understand what happened and remember your friend or family member. Denying the loss is an easy way to isolate yourself and will frustrate your support system in the process. Another way to cope is to accept your feelings. People experience all kinds of emotions after the death of someone close. Sadness, anger, frustration and even exhaustion are all normal.

Taking care of yourself and your family is an important step in healing from grief. Eating well, exercising and getting plenty of rest will help you get through each day and move forward. Reach out and help others dealing with loss. It can be an added benefit of making you feel better as well as someone else that may be going through something similar. One thing I found to be very helpful for me is to remember and celebrate the lives of your loved ones. You can do this by donating to a favorite charity of the deceased, framing photos of fun times, passing on a family name to a baby or planting a garden in their memory.

What you choose is up to you, as long as it allows you to honor that unique relationship in a way that feels right to you. If you are feeling stuck or overwhelmed by emotions, it may be helpful to talk to a licensed psychologist or mental health professional who can help you cope with your feelings and find ways to get you back on track.

I would say that the death of my father really stuck with me. Even though he was going through the illness and suffering from cancer, I believed that there would be a way and he would pull through. During the weeks leading up to his passing, I watched him suffer pain where he barely wanted to talk or do anything. He just wanted to sleep. There were times when I could hear him cry out, "Lord, take me now," because the pain was so excruciating. The weekend before his passing, I was with him, and when I left to drive back home, I had a feeling that was the last time I would see my dad. Part of me wanted to believe that a miracle could happen, but two days later, I was sitting in a training session and received a call from my mother at 11:27 a.m. that my dad was gone at 11:24 a.m. When I first got the news, I was shocked. I was walking around, and then I told my manager that I had to leave, my father passed, and I didn't cry. My manager was concerned and didn't want me to take the subway, so he drove me to my car, and I didn't say a word.

Once I got home, I started packing my bags and then called my brother and a few of my closest friends. When I spoke to my brother, he asked if I was going to drive down to North Carolina. I remember telling him, "Yes, how else was I going to get there?" So, I tried to pack but I couldn't figure out what to pack, and I broke down. I couldn't believe that I was packing for my dad's funeral. I got myself together and proceeded to drive down from Maryland to North Carolina.

It took about four hours, and when I arrived at the family home, my mom and Aunt Pawnee were there. There were a few other people leaving, and I walked into the room where my father died. I didn't cry; I was angry. I was feeling a sense of anger. I immediately put myself into a busy mode, planning the funeral, reaching out to family, and doing everything I needed to do to make sure my mom had everything she needed. If you've ever had to plan a funeral before for a close family member, then you know that there is a viewing before the actual wake and funeral. Funeral homes have a viewing for the family members to view the body and ensure that they are pleased with the results of the preparation of the body. When we got to the viewing, I cried some, but I didn't break down like I thought. I was still in a state of disbelief. I felt like my dad was coming back and this was temporary, like when he went to the hospital, he came home.

During the funeral, I didn't cry. My brother cried, but I was very serious. I talked to my cousins and family members during the repast, took a few pictures, and went home. After the repast, many of my cousins came to the family house and sat around, talking about my dad and the funny things they remembered of him. During that time, I was okay. Just having some of those cousins around made me feel good, and my inner-self believed I was just at a family function and my dad was going to show up. It wasn't until after everyone left that the grief really hit hard.

The idea of not being able to talk to my dad bothered me for some time. You see, I am a daddy's girl. I talked to my father all the time.

I talked to him about everything from work, business, money, car, and just telling him what I was going to do. When my parents moved back to North Carolina, I called every week and spoke to them. My mom would answer the phone, I would ask her how she was doing, and she would respond, and then I would say, "Put daddy on the phone," or she already knew, and sometimes she would say, "You want to speak to your dad?" So, the fact that I couldn't talk to him anymore was hurtful. I literally didn't know how I was going to get through life without talking things over with my dad. There were times when he was so sick and he would tell me that he might not make it, and I would continue to encourage him and say, "You are going to make it, because one day, you will have to walk me down the aisle." He would say, "You may have to get your brother to do it." Hearing that made my heart drop.

Losing my father affected me in so many ways, from my thoughts on how I do things to relationships. When my father passed, I didn't want to go to the family home. Often times, I didn't want to talk to my mother. It just reminded me of my dad. The house still had my dad's clothing. His hats and his cars were still in the driveway. It was the same as how he left it, and my mother didn't want to change things around, so it was difficult to come into the house. It took almost a year to gather up all of his clothes and give them away. My mom depended on me to do everything, so that added to some of the stress, which is probably why I didn't want to talk to her sometimes because I knew she needed something. My father did all the work around the house. He paid the bills; he took care of his family—he was a good man. I know my mom missed him after being married to him for over forty years. It was like after he died, I had to take care of everything, and it was a lot to deal with emotionally. Eventually, I talked to some counselors at my church and was able to get my mind thinking more positive. The first few years were difficult; I would find myself crying to sleep or tearing up if I had a question for my dad that he couldn't answer.

When you lose your parents as an adult, there's often much to do, such as contacting relatives, planning the memorial and funeral and sorting through possessions. The reality is you are swept up in the busyness, and then in about three months to a year, it really hits. And it's usually about that time when the support has moved on; all the family and friends that were there have gone home and back to their own lives. The family traditions change as the first holidays and birthdays pass without them. The second year is the year we realize they're never coming back. We're never seeing them again; it's just us now.

Time does not heal all wounds, but the pain of loss does lessen with time. Don't expect yourself to quickly recover, and don't feel there is anything abnormal about intense feelings of grief. It can be comforting spending time with others who've gone through a similar loss, whether it's friends or strangers in a support group. My church has a bereavement ministry, and I reached out to someone from that group and attended a few of their meetings. I believe it helped with me moving forward. Sharing grief online helped some. I posted a photo of my father on the anniversary of his death and on his birthday. Even though it helped me, I didn't realize how it would make my brother feel. Years later, I talked to him about it, and he admitted that seeing the photos online sometimes made him feel sad. So, when posting, it is important to keep others in mind. But I noticed that when others online see what you are going through you find out they have been through something as well, so you end up encouraging them during their grieving process. It's okay to grieve and allow others to see it because if you isolate yourself, you can become depressed or bitter.

This work of grief takes time; the process must not be hurried. And it is never entirely over. Even as an adult, don't be surprised by feelings of abandonment and uncertainty that you experience. I felt alone. Although my mom and brother were here, I just wanted to talk to my dad. Grief does not end; it comes and goes, and then it comes again. If you feel the need, seek out support from others who've been there, a friend who cares, or a professional who can help guide you through the work of grief.

I hope sharing my story about grief can help others whether you lost a parent, friend, or close relative. It will help in the healing. And know you're not the first one, and you definitely won't be the last to experience this pain.

Everything Has Its Time

To everything *there is* a season,
A time for every purpose under heaven: A time to be born,
And a time to die; A time to plant,
And a time to pluck *what is* planted;
A time to kill, and a time to heal;
A time to break down, and a time to build up;
A time to weep, And a time to laugh;
A time to mourn And a time to dance;
A time to cast away stones,
And a time to gather stones;
A time to embrace,
And a time to refrain from embracing;
A time to gain, And a time to lose;
A time to keep, And a time to throw away;
And a time to sew;
A time to keep silence,
And a time to speak;
A time to love, And a time to hate;
A time of war, And a time of peace.
Ecclesiastes 3:1-8

Chapter Eight *Food for thought* on *Grief is a Journey*

List some things you liked to do with your loved one.

How can you use the items listed to continue to celebrate that loved one.

CHAPTER 9

The Temple I Choose to Live

Being healthy is very important. In 2018, I had a little health scare when I was diagnosed with Atrial Fibrillation, also known as AFIB. Here I am in my forties, and my doctor diagnosed me with something he said people ages sixty and over have. AFIB is a condition when your heart's normal rhythm is out of whack because your blood isn't moving well, and you are at risk of heart failure. It's when your heart can't keep up with your body's needs, and the blood can also pool inside your heart and form clots. If one gets stuck in your brain, you can have a stroke. So, this whole thing had me on edge. I did not know how I got this, and I was not trying to get a stroke. After the diagnosis, my doctor put me on some aspirin, and within two weeks, I was in the hospital for internal bleeding from taking the aspirin.

All of this led to me making changes in my health, first by getting rid of the high blood pressure, which can lead to the AFIB. I started trying to eat the right foods, but that wasn't enough. Why does it take something to happen to us before we decide to change our lifestyles? I refuse to be part of the generational curse of diabetes, high blood pressure and obesity, to name a few things that run in my family.

What does being healthy mean? Well, to me, it means feeling fit, strong and confident. Being realistic and doing what works for you and your body, eating a balanced diet with wholesome foods, and enjoying the occasional treat when you feel like it. Physical activity helps to prevent some risks such as hypertension, diabetes, and heart disease. It also helps to improve muscle and bone health and sleep.

Being healthy is a state of complete physical, mental and social well-being, not the absence of disease or infirmity. Having good nutrition is an important part of leading a healthy lifestyle. When will you take a stand on your health? Combined with physical activity, your diet can help you to reach and maintain a healthy weight, reduce your risk of chronic diseases like heart disease and cancer, and promote your overall good health.

If there's one thing I hate doing, it's exercising. I was not good with committing to exercise. I would start out with a thirty-minute work-out, but I would not stay consistent. After a few weeks, the workouts would stop. After my health scare, I pushed myself to get fit, and that became my motivation. I hired a personal trainer and was able to commit to at least four workouts a week. I'm still not an exercise lover, but I have made a commitment to myself to get off the blood pressure medicine and become more active. I choose to live!

Staying healthy physically can help you stay healthy emotionally. If you are eating the right food and keeping fit, your body will be strong, and it will help you to cope with stress and anxiety and also fight illness. When it comes to exercising, I actually find ways to motivate myself other than the fact that I have to work out to lower my blood pressure. After you do something for twenty-one days, it becomes a habit. You can also get a partner. Sometimes having some-one else to work out with will motivate you. Start setting goals, not just to lose weight, but just fitness goals. Once you start exercising and see yourself change, you will want to continue.

Stop making up excuses. You have to fight for your life. Once I started exercising regularly, I wasn't concerned about my hair; I just made it work. I wear a hairstyle that is low-maintenance and manageable after workouts.

Choosing to live a healthy lifestyle is a choice to develop and maintain healthy eating habits and engage in regular exercise. It's not a decision that you make once in a lifetime and then forget. You can live a healthy lifestyle by making the decision to do so.

The trick to making your lifestyle healthier is to make small, healthy changes every day, such as taking the steps instead of the elevator, increasing your fruit by one piece and drinking water. The body is truly the temple of the soul, and you don't want that temple to fall apart! Exercise is a great way to stimulate your health. Physical activity helps improve longevity and overall health. For exercise, you can start out with walking for fifteen minutes, then increase to thirty minutes that you can work into your daily routine. You can pick a convenient time in your schedule. You could exercise for thirty minutes the morning to get energized for your day. Before going to a trainer, I felt like exercising was more of a chore that I had to do. For me, working out with a trainer and in small groups helps keep me motivated through the exercises. If you remember to keep your workouts fun, you should enjoy it and not feel like it's a chore. Some fun physical activities include dancing, Zumba, yoga, aerobics, running, and even hiking.

Maintaining the temple also includes eating fruits and vegetables. Adding fruits and vegetables is a perfect foundation for starting a healthy routine. Vegetables, like leafy greens, and fruits contain plentiful nutrients such as vitamins and antioxidants that help boost your immune system and fight off disease-causing toxins. Antioxidants help fight eye disease and promote healthy skin and overall health.

Drink plenty of water; it will improve your health throughout the day. The natural liquid offers the benefits of hydration, nourishment, and improved well-being. Water can cleanse toxins from the body, improve brain function, energize muscles, control weight gain, and balance body temperature and fluids.

When it comes to building a healthy lifestyle, it's easy to concentrate on the physical aspects of health and ignore the mental upkeep. Your mental health is the foundation of your overall health. It's important to manage and asses your feelings on a day-to-day basis. If you feel negative towards others, you could cause more unhappiness at work, school, or in your social life. De-stress yourself. Sometimes it's beneficial to stop, take a deep breath, and relax. You can help maintain your physical and mental health by decompressing from a long, stressful school or workweek. Try some relaxing activities to help you unwind. Take advantage of meditation, listening to music, reading, watching a comedy, or exercising.

Taking care of the Temple is not just about eating the right foods and exercising; it includes keeping your exterior clean as well. When you look good and smell good, you feel good. When you leave your home, you want to make sure your hair is combed and you are clean. You should have on clean clothes and smell fresh and clean.

It is important to address any concerns you have with your body once you realize something is wrong. The sooner you know something is wrong, the sooner it can be healed and resolved. If you feel a lump in your breast or anywhere else that you normally would not find a lump, you need to address that issue. When I went for my annual routine women's wellness exam in early December, my doctor told me that my heart sounded like it was beating irregularly. She told me to have my primary care physician to take a look right away. So, I scheduled the appointment for the next month in January.

When I made it to my doctor the following month and she checked my heart, she asked me if I noticed something different about myself. I told her that I had been out of breath a lot when just walking or going up the stairs in my house. And I told her that my heart had been beating very fast. She told me that I was lucky I didn't have a stroke. She started to run an electrocardiogram also known as an EKG. This EKG test is used to detect and study heart problems such as heart attacks, arrhythmia or irregular heartbeat and heart failure. After running the test, my readings were far from normal. I was surprised, I was nervous, and I was scared.

My doctor started asking me questions like how long had this been going on, and I told her since I went to my annual Women's Wellness check in December. The doctor told me to see my primary right away because she heard an irregular heartbeat when listening through the stethoscope. My doctor said I should have scheduled an appointment right away. I had all of these excuses: holidays, and so on, and I didn't have time. My doctor immediately called a cardiologist, and with me sitting there, she started talking to the cardiologist and telling him my symptoms and readings from the EKG test. After she got off the phone, she gave me an aspirin right there, prescribed blood pressure medicine, and put me on an aspirin regimen. I say all this to say, don't ignore the signs. If something is going on with you and body, act on it. Don't put it off. I don't know what would have happened if I didn't go to my doctor when I did, but all I can say is that I am still here through the grace of God.

Your body is your temple! You must take care of yourself. If you can do anything that can prevent something from happening to you, you need to do that. Stop playing! I listen to my friends all the time who tell me about something that's wrong with them, but they haven't been to the doctor to get it checked out. What are you waiting for? The entire ordeal had me shook! The heart is a major organ of the body, and if it stops, I'm gone! So, I wanted to do everything I could to keep it healthy. Also, with a family history of heart disease, and with my Dad having several heart attacks, I was very much concerned and wanted everything healed as soon as possible. I witnessed my dad having a heart attack on Christmas day. Christmas was never the same after that. I remember being awakened by my mother asking me to take my father to the hospital because he was having chest pains. We spent Christmas Day in the hospital because my father's chest pains turned out to be a heart attack.

There was one instance when I was in middle school—I may have been eleven or twelve years old—and it was during the time I was out of school during summer break. I received a call from my father, and he told me to call his boss and let them know he would not be at work that day because he was in the hospital. I called his boss and told him what my father told me to say. I really didn't know what was going on, so I decided to walk up to the hospital. I grabbed my best friend whose mother also worked at the same hospital and we went up there. Children weren't allowed in the visitation area, so we went into the hospital as if we were visiting my best friend Rhonda's mother, Mrs. Patton, who worked there. Once I got to Mrs. Patton, I told her my father was in the hospital and I wanted to see him. I didn't know what was wrong with him, so Mrs. Patton was able to tell me where to find my father, and I ended up in the intensive care unit (ICU) where my father was hooked up to many machines. The nurse wasn't going to let me see him, but I was persistent about talking to my father. When I saw him, I cried and asked why he was there, and he told me he had a heart attack.

My heart was broken. I was scared because my father took care of everything for our family. He worked hard and made sure we were taken care of. It was from that point that I learned about heart disease and the seriousness of it. My father, along with a few of his siblings, had heart disease, including my paternal grandfather who died from a heart attack. So, you see, that is why that concern sits heavy on my heart. I don't want to be susceptible to a generational curse.

Your body is your temple, so you want to maintain it. It needs rest, both in the physical (sleep and taking breaks) and spiritual (resting in the presence of God in worship, prayer and fasting). Give your body a break. It's wise to eat healthier food always. Feed your body with the right kinds of food, but know that alone is not enough. We should also eat in moderation so that we are eating just the right amounts of food. Too much sodium, oil, sugar, and other things can be very dangerous to our health.

As I mentioned earlier, give your body exercise. Also, respect yourself as a body that God made. Brothers, this means treating the human body the way God wants us to. Women aren't to be lusted after; they're to be respected. We shouldn't measure a woman by her vital statistics (butt, breast, and body shape). Sisters, the same goes for you. Don't treat your body as if it's something you need to flash to gain attention and praise. You aren't measured by your physical beauty. Finally, don't compare your body to others. When you catch yourself comparing your body to the bodies of others, do not beat yourself up or tell yourself you should not be doing that. Instead, use it as an opportunity to love yourself. You are unique and the one and only you.

Chapter Nine *Food for thought* The Temple

What does being healthy mean to you?

Have you noticed anything physically wrong with your body? If so, what are you going to do about it? Are you going to tell your doctor or just wait and see what happens?

CHAPTER 10

Friends Make Us Who We Are

A good friend is a perfect person to bounce your ideas off of and share your dreams, frustrations and fears. Friends provide a safety zone where you don't have to worry about being judged and you feel free to be yourself. Friends often serve as free personal therapists as they often patiently listen to our thoughts, fears and real-life dramas.

Friendship is important to me, and I know that people come into your life for a reason. Sometimes it's a good thing and sometimes it's toxic. When I was a young girl in middle school, I had a few friends, but back then I don't think that I realized the true meaning of friendship. I didn't understand it until I matured into a young adult. What is a friend? I mean, what is a true friend to you? A friend is someone who lets you have total freedom to be yourself. Whatever you happen to be feeling at the moment is fine with them. Your friends will tell you the truth even if you don't want to hear it. They stand by your side no matter what you are going through.

All of your friends aren't the same; they are very different, and your reason for being their friend may be different from another. When I was in middle school, I had a best friend named Rhonda. We hung out together, went to concerts together—we did everything together. Her parents and siblings knew me and mine knew her. If one of us went somewhere, the other one had to go, and we always had to return home together. When we entered high school, we accumulated other friends. Rhonda had a set of friends and I had some too, and when we hung out, we didn't always hang out together because we had a separate set of friends. But at the end of the day, if Rhonda or I wanted to go somewhere important, her mom would always ask if I was going, and my parents would ask if Rhonda was going with me. We went to New Edition concerts and we also went to see Prince. Our parents trusted us to be with one another and that we would not get ourselves into trouble.

Once we finished high school, we lost touch and went on to separate colleges and didn't see each other much anymore. It didn't mean we weren't friends anymore; we were still friends, but we matured and had different interests which kept us doing different things. I can't recall what brought us together as friends during middle school, but Rhonda and I are two totally different people. Rhonda was loud, outspoken, and funny. She was somewhat of an extrovert, while I was more of an introvert: quiet, soft-spoken, and funny too. As teenagers, we both liked to have fun. I remember one time we were looking for summer jobs at a local mall, but no one was hiring. We both wanted to work so we could earn some extra money for clothes. Well, that day we didn't find a job, but we came home with some clothes that we found. We did things on the edge, hoping our parents wouldn't find out some things we did because we both knew we would be in trouble. Although we are adults now living in different states and living separate lives, we don't see each other much, but we can reminisce about the fun times we had. We were both able to be ourselves around one another, and that's what made us best friends during those teenage years.

During childhood, sometimes your cousins become your first friends. They are usually the first set of kids you play with at every family function. I am the youngest grandchild of my paternal grandmother. As I was growing up, most of my first cousins were old enough to be my parents, so when there was a family event, I would play with their children—my second cousins. I have a few cousin-friends that I am close with and trust as if they were my friends. We have a bond like no other. We share the same opinions about certain family members, and we have common favorite relatives that we love to talk to and visit. Cousin-friends don't judge each other. They judge other people together. They literally have known you since day one and understand you. Now, I'm talking about cousin-friends, not all cousins. Your cousin always has your best interests at heart, which is why they will be brutally honest with you because they always want you to have the best of everything.

Friends may come and go, but cousin-friends are for life. They will love you and cherish you forever. Words fall short to describe the special bond we share with our cousins. They are a big part of so many of our childhood memories, family pictures and life in general. You can afford to be stupid with them, talk nonsense and have that nonsense respected. And if you get lucky enough, they are also your best friends forever. I know when my cousin-friends read this, they will know who they are, and there's more than one of them.

As I have grown into a young woman, I have established friendships with a lot of people, but there are only a few that I can truly say are my best of friends. Some are associates, and some are not friends at all. It's important that I am a true friend to my friends. I believe I have the characteristics of a true friend, such as companionship and affection. I give my friends emotional support and I contribute positively to their lives. It is important to have positive people in your life, so if your so-called friend is giving you negative feedback, lying to you or talking about you behind your back, then they are not a friend.

I have friends that have been part of my life for over twenty years. In the early part of 2014, I found out that one of my dear friend's Va'Nechia's cancer had returned. I was in town for a family event, so I stayed with my friend Vee, as we affectionately called her, and she explained that she would be starting treatment the following week, and everything would be okay. As we stayed up all night talking and catching up on each other's lives, she would always say what a great friend I was to her. When she was in the hospital during a previous cancer fight, I went to see her, and she was so weak that she could barely talk. So, I sat there for at least two hours and talked to her until she started laughing. She remembered that moment the night I came to visit, and she told me that when I came to see her, she was not feeling well, and she was in so much pain that she didn't want to talk to anyone. But my visit lifted her spirits, and I made her laugh so hard that she could ignore the pain.

When she told me that story, I didn't think much of it at the time and just figured she was reminiscing, but she was telling me in her own way how I have always been a great friend. Va'Nechia passed away in April 2014, and I couldn't believe that my friend for over twenty years had died. You see, I would call her superwoman. She was married and had three daughters (two were twins); she was a working woman and was very active at her church. I always admired her poise, strength, and passion for life. Va'Nechia was like a big sister to me, and losing her just broke my heart. Her family asked me to speak at her funeral about friendship. I have never spoken in front of a large crowd like that, especially in a church pulpit. I prepared some notes and topics on what I was going to talk about in regard to friendship. I started to talk about our friendship, and the next thing I knew, people were laughing. As I told some stories about Va'Nechia and me, it started to feel like I was really celebrating her life and I felt her presence. Telling the stories about Va'Nechia and me, about how I was that friend to her, she was that sister-friend to me, and the effect her friendship had on me speaks volumes. She set the bar for true friends. When and if I ever get married and have children, I am going to be that "Superwoman" wife, mother, daughter, and friend, just like Va'Nechia.

True friends want to see you do well. They are fans of what you do, and you are the same to them. It's important to recognize who your true friends are and only surround yourself with people like them. A true friend is going to tell you, "Girl, that hair is a mess," or "That dress looks good on you." True friends are not jealous of your success; they are cheerleaders. True friends are honest. They will tell you the truth about what's going on with them. They don't lie to your face. True friends are loyal. They don't talk about you behind your back and then smile in your face. There have been people in my life who claimed they were friends, but when I was not around, they would be talking about me, jealous of what I had or how I looked.

As I mentioned earlier, you can have different types of friends for different reasons. All of your friends are different. You can have friends of the opposite sex, meaning that you are not having sex with them and they are not your ex-boyfriend or ex-girlfriend, and they are not expecting an intimate relationship with you. I can't really say I have a true male best friend, but I do have acquaintances. Either way, if they are not spreading positive energy, then they have no room in my life.

Friendships are beneficial and can help reduce stress. When you are in a bad relationship or friendship, it can cause you unnecessary stress. We hope that we enjoy our relationships and can draw on them when we need support, whether that be practical support like a workout or running buddy, going out to eat or going for a walk or emotional support, like when you need to vent about something going on in your life or you just need a shoulder to cry on.

We tend to spend time more so with friends than we do with our immediate families. Friendship is a relationship of enjoyment and convenience, whereas spousal or family relationships have their share of negative emotions, and some stay together out of a sense of obligation. If you have hundreds and thousands of friends on social media, they are not your true friends. They may be a combination of friends, family, co-workers, associates, classmates and others, but I can only count on my true friends to call me when I need to talk, not send me a message on social media or a text message.

Having just one friend who loves and supports you can be more beneficial than having a long list of acquaintances.

If your friend lies to you, no matter if it's about little things or big things, chances are you don't have a true friendship. Find out if they gossip about you. If you feel like your friend is always gossiping about someone or talking trash, chances are your "friend" will do the same as soon as your back is turned. Showing up for weddings, baby showers, and other important events in your friend's life is a big part of the job. There may be times when conflicts in your schedule prevent you from being there in person, but your friend needs to know that you are supportive when it counts. If you find yourself constantly making excuses to skip out on these occasions, you may want to take a look at the reasons why.

We all want our friends to succeed. But it shouldn't be a competition. Part of being friends is rooting for one another and celebrating each other's wins. Constantly trying to outdo the other person is petty, and it's a sign that your friendship isn't as solid as it could be.

Relationships require compromise, and friendships are no exception. You and your friends won't always see eye to eye, but that doesn't have to mean that the relationship is in trouble. Whether it's what movie you're going to see or what new restaurant you're going to try on Friday night, you should be willing to give a little from time to time. Everything doesn't always have to be your way or the highway.

Friends can help you feel better emotionally and physically. Whether you're having a bad day, need care while at home ill, or just going through a rough time, having a friend around to lift your spirits can do the body and soul good. Even when it comes to mental illnesses, friends can make a difference. For example, if you are going through depression, a healthy mood around you can be a good thing. Your friends can protect you from depression and possibly help you recover from it.

Friends who show they care help improve the quality of your life overall. Having friends is having someone who truly sees and hears you. So many of the relationships in our lives require us to play a role such as a parent, daughter, sibling, spouse, boss, employee, and the list can go on. But with friends, you just get to be you. Our friends can help us navigate the many different stages of life in a way that no other relationship can. My friend Va'Nechia was very influential to me. She was a godly woman, and she was always kind. The way she responded to or handled situations, and through her advice, I observed the right way to conduct myself during a time in my life when I was a confused young woman.

Trust is a key element of all friendships; however, it really must be a two-way street. Friendship involves being open and honest, and, as a result, provides opportunities that teach you both how to trust others and, in turn, how to be trustworthy. You don't have to worry about a true friend talking behind your back because she won't do that. She'll stick up for you even when you're not there. A friend is someone that you can confide in with complete trust. A friend is someone you respect and that respects you, and that respect is not based upon worthiness but is based upon like-mindedness.

Friends make us feel connected in a way that provides us with a deep sense of comfort, identity and belonging. Just knowing that you have someone you can call when you need a hand or shoulder to lean on provides each of us with a sense of contentment and peace of mind. Even though some people are much more social than others, we all tend to need honest and personal interactions with others at certain times. Friends supply the perfect anti-loneliness remedy by allowing us to feel like a part of something bigger.

Having friends around gives you encouragement. Even now as an adult, you can never stop learning how to be a better person. One thing I value most in life is friends. They will support you even at times you may be afraid to admit that you need help. Surround yourself with good, true friends who celebrate your successes, and know that no matter what you do, you are not alone. Good friends can make you feel healthier and happier; they give you strength and courage. Everyone deserves to have a true friend.

Friendship is a gift from God ...a friend loves at all times.
(Proverbs 17:17)

Chapter Ten *Food for thought* on Friendship

What does true friendship mean to you?

How can you be a better friend?

Do you trust all your friends? Why? Or Why not?

CHAPTER 11

Unbreakable

EVERYDAY GRACE: LIVING THE LIFE YOU WERE BORN TO LIVE

You are unbreakable; you are unstoppable. "Everyday Grace" is living your life in the midst of adversity, despite your troubles. It means you are destined for greatness and experiencing the full gift of God. The Word of God says that it is not by law but by grace that we meet the Lord and walk with the Lord. How do you live by grace? One way to live day-by-day by His grace is to have humility. The self-sufficient and self-reliant are not looking for the grace of God. In their pride, they do not work in that flowing supply of riches of the grace of God. God resists and is opposed to the proud. Those who think they can handle it by their own best efforts or resources will be broken so that God may properly bless them with life in His grace. Humility is vital in living day-by-day by the grace of God. Humility is central to our recognition that we need God's grace daily. God is ready to pour out his grace upon, in, and through us.

Also essential to living in the grace of God is faith. Faith is the intimate partner with humility, for both are necessary to the abounding life of grace God promises. Humility says, "I need help." Faith says, "I can trust God for that help." Faith is trusting God in the quietest of times; it is trusting God in the most chaotic of times; it is trusting God in times of inaction, and it is trusting God when you are battling hard until you cannot imagine possibly taking another step.

Paying Attention to Everyday Grace & Joy

If we pay attention to things going on around us, we can live meaningful lives in our community with others. It's not just paying attention to general things; it's actually looking out for moments of grace and joy. There are plenty of things out there that if we pay attention exclusively to them, they will allow us to lose confidence and hope, and they will tempt us to believe there is little that is good and beautiful in the world. Not only are these elements before us, but there is an entire media and news industry that seeks to draw these things to our attention. This means that we actually have to work at paying attention to joy, beauty and grace. When we notice some of the amazing things all around us in the ordinary, such as an evening of laughter with a friend, a shared secret, a hug just when we need it, the delight of watching young children at play, the warmth of the sun after a week of rain, snow, and clouds, we are reoriented from threat to possibility and from despair to joy.

The point is that every single one of us can not only lead richer lives but also encourage those around us by looking for the amazing "coincidences" of grace that surround us. But we need to pay attention, look for them, lift them up and give thanks for them. Have you ever noticed how much you enjoy being around a person who sees the possibilities in almost every situation and relentlessly looks for good in the people they are around? Believe it or not, you can be one of those people!

Sustaining and Growing in Grace

When we opened our hearts to God's saving grace, we began a relationship with God that He wants to continue throughout our lives. God's saving grace should be followed by His sanctifying grace. The word sanctify means "to set apart, to make holy or healthy." God not only sees who we are, but He sees who we can become through His growing grace. God did not bring you into His kingdom for you to remain as you are, but to grow.

God has given his children the grace to endure unbelievable hardships. We see this throughout Scripture. Grace may be defined not only as God's unmerited favor but also as the power of God, which He gives us to sustain and help us in every time of need. Some ways to apply God's sustaining grace to painful moments in your life are first to develop the habit of comparing your pain with those who hurt more than you do, rather than with those who hurt less than you do. Also, remind yourself of the short nature of your trial. One of the worst things that you can do when going through a painful trial is to freeze that moment in time. Do not focus on it as if there were never good things that preceded it or as if it will never end.

Become unbreakable; create a personal self-resilience to be unstoppable! We cannot escape pain, difficulty, failure, tragedy, and heartache. Sooner or later, it will find us, despite our best efforts to protect ourselves. Instead of trying to bob and weave around what life throws at us, I'd rather have the comfort of knowing that I can take life's best shot and be able to get back up and move forward. To me, that's empowerment. Having that kind of personal fortitude and resilience is a game-changer. Instead of being dogged by fear and uncertainty, you will have inner peace and confidence that you will survive.

I mentioned this earlier, and I may be sounding redundant, but you have to make connections. Personal resilience doesn't mean it's all up to you. Having good relationships with close family members, friends, or others is critical to resilience and well-being. When tragedy strikes, the worst thing you can do is avoid friends and loved ones. You have a whole network of people that can help you. Avoid seeing a crisis as an insurmountable problem. Don't fall into the trap of all-or-nothing thinking, which says that everything is either perfect or terrible. There are always shades of gray.

Focus less on the past and more on the future you want. Accept that change is a part of living. Know that whatever you're going through, others have experienced before. You are not alone. Change, in whatever form, is a natural part of life. Move toward your goals. When the present is difficult, focus on a better future. What do you want your life to be? What goals do you have that you can start moving toward? Take decisive actions; avoid checking out by taking whatever control you have over your situation and doing something about it. Look for opportunities for self-discovery. I'm sure you've heard the saying, "Sometimes you win, and sometimes you learn." Tragedy and pain can be an opportunity to re-evaluate your life, where you've been, and where you want to go.

Ask yourself the tough questions and look for ways to grow. Nurture a positive view of yourself. Be careful how you talk to yourself. Don't accept blame when it isn't warranted. Focus on your strengths and abilities to get you through. Keep things in perspective. When something bad happens, it can change all aspects of your life. Your job is to put it into perspective. Don't let one bad event taint your view of the other areas in your life. Maintain a hopeful outlook, and just watch how you explain or think about your situation. When possible, take a more positive and optimistic view.

Increase your tolerance for pain. If you want to train your mind effectively in becoming resilient, you need to increase your tolerance for pain. You do it by letting go of how things should be and accept what is. No expectations, no feeling of entitlement. When you feel entitled to something better or easier in life, you are putting yourself in a position where your expectations don't have to be met. This situation causes hurt and loss of control. When you are at peace with the ups and downs of life, knowing that some fights are involved, you are gaining more control over how you feel and think. Your tolerance for adversity increases since you are focused more on a solution than on the presence of your pain.

Learn to be alone. Some of us are pretty scared of being alone. That's why we keep the TV on even when we don't watch it, scroll through our social media feed fifty times a day, or always seek some company just to maintain the noise. Spending some time alone allows you to think clearly, without distractions and on a much deeper level. Now, I am not suggesting that you isolate yourself from others, but time alone, combined with only five minutes of meditation, will help you in gaining better control of your feelings and overall mental state. Schedule your alone time. Reserve one hour, twice a week, just for yourself, your thoughts and feelings. If you haven't tried meditation, there are tons of videos online which will teach you the basics.

Love those who hurt you. I know that's hard to grasp, but think about it this way: when you truly let go, when you forgive, you are gaining more control over your feelings and mindset. And that's one of the most important things in building mental resilience. You take away the power of someone else who gained it through hurting you. Once you overcome the feeling of anger and the need for retaliation, the action of the other person won't control you.

Now, as you are becoming unbreakable, you can be unstoppable and successful. To get ahead in your career or seek out a new job, you need a high level of self-confidence. I talked about self-confidence in an earlier chapter, but I feel like you need to know you can be successful in your career. To be unstoppable, I would suggest things like waking up earlier. If you could just start waking up a little earlier, and put first things first, then your interactions with others would change. Also, you will have time to do the things you need to do. If you wake up late or oversleep, you missed a good part of the morning to accomplish your tasks.

Turn off the television (this is one thing I struggle with). The television is a big distraction. Once you start watching a show, you don't stop, or you get caught up in some movie, and the next thing you know, it's late-night and time for bed. The next thing is to put down your phone, turn it off, or put it in airplane mode. You can use screens to entertain yourself and produce amazing work. But that work, although interesting and important, should produce a better quality of life in the real world for you. How much time do you spend staring at the screen? You are wasting a lot of valuable time. Set goals, write them down, and work toward manifesting and achieving them every single day. Write them down in the morning and check them off throughout the day as you complete them.

Being unstoppable is to keep physically, mentally and emotionally fit to power through the tough times. Surround yourself with smart, positive, upbeat and enthusiastic people. In your career, always stay alert and keep your eyes and ears open to learn about the next great opportunity. If you are interested in doing something, research and find out the tools you need to do it.

Take care of yourself. Do what you can to sleep well and eat well. Try to get some exercise and do things you enjoy. If you feel like nothing is enjoyable, do things that make you feel less horrible. In short, be nice to yourself.

Being unbreakable doesn't mean that you can't cry or need to act tough or mask your feelings by putting on a happy face. Being unbreakable means you give yourself the freedom to break, knowing you have the tools to put yourself back together again.

Never stop, never quit, and never give up.

In conclusion, living every day by grace means God works in us, and God works with us by His grace for fruit, good works, and obedience. A great and benedictory response of humility of faith to God's grace for daily living works in us. Remember to pay attention to God's everyday grace and joy.

Chapter Eleven *Food for thought* on *Unbreakable*

What is stopping you from being unbreakable? What do you want your life to be? What goals do you have that you can start moving toward?

CHAPTER 12

Obstacles Are Your Path to Opportunity

There are many things that happen in our lives that put us off the course that we were on. Obstacles that would cause us to slow down, experience stress, or give up completely. What we do not realize is that sometimes what feels like major setbacks and obstacles in our lives can turn into transformative opportunities if we allow them to be. Sometimes obstacles actually allow us the opportunity to reflect on how we could do things differently and examine what did and did not work right the first time around. Obstacles can also open up time and opportunity that we did not once have. Time to decide on goals, time to learn a new skill or time to complete tasks that feel like you never had the time to do prior to this obstacle coming into your life.

What have you always wanted to do? What have you not had the time to accomplish before? Another amazing opportunity that obstacles allow us is the gift of reflection and hindsight. Did a project that you were working on just not seem to work? Did you test run a program or workshop and received some difficult to hear, but important to know, feedback? Obstacles and stumbles allow us to go back to the drawing board and rethink how things could have gone differently. What was it that went wrong? What was the common feedback that you received that people did not like? These are obstacles, not failures. Things did not go as planned, but you received the rare gift of being able to see and hear what did not work. You now have the chance to go back to the drawing board to make this product, this program, this presentation, everything that people wanted it to be. The end result may be something that is hugely successful, where the starting product could be the end of something really big.

One of the greatest gifts of obstacles and setbacks is the chance to do things you may never have made the leap to do otherwise. Have you been laid off and had time on your hands, or were you passed over for that promotion that you were putting in extra hours killing yourself to get? This new free time in your schedule, or new reasons to finally consider your options is such an opportunity for you. Take the scary leap and branch out on your own in your profession. If you have weeks of time on your hands, take that training class you have been dreaming of doing. Not only does it build your skill base, but you may learn something you love. Take this time to set some challenging and exciting goals for yourself. This is your chance to really think about these things on a level that you may have felt unable to before. Why is this all possible? Because you chose to embrace your obstacles as opportunities. The possibilities are endless.

There are ways to transform your obstacles into opportunities for success. Some I may have mentioned in earlier chapters, but I just want it to resonate with you. One thing you do is keep your energy positive. When things get tough, it's important to stay positive. Your emotions directly affect your thinking. Freaking out will not help the situation; it will have your mind thinking crazy and make it more difficult to look for solutions. Obstacles are unavoidable, but it's better to spend your days working through them from a positive state of mind than to affect your well-being by feeling terrible for however long the obstacle lasts. Remember that you're allowed to enjoy the journey. It's absolutely okay to struggle and to smile while you're doing so. By staying positive, you can approach obstacles with a clear mind, curiosity, and lack of judgment. You'll be able to find a solution more quickly and feel good in the process. We can't always control events, but we can control our attitude. Choose an attitude to prevail. Develop an unshakable belief in yourself and your abilities. Have the confidence to be the exception that overcomes all obstacles: someone who is willing to bet on themselves.

Another way to transform your obstacles into opportunities is to ask for help graciously. Do not be afraid to ask for help, and, more importantly, be gracious to everyone, regardless of whether they are the cause of or solution to your obstacle. Taking your frustration out on those around you will only result in disgruntled employees, spouses, and friends. Your difficult situation is probably not their fault, and even if it is, you don't want anyone feeling resistant towards helping you solve it. You are as strong as your support system, so make sure you're creating an environment where the right people want to help you. Even when you're the one who needs help, do whatever is within your power to meet people halfway. When transforming obstacles into opportunities, you may need to become persistent and solutions-oriented. Most problems have more than one solution, and the more we actively train ourselves to look for them, the quicker we become at finding them. To transcend your problem, invite this higher mind to create the best possible solution without forming attachments to how and when it makes its way into your life. All answers to problems exist on a level of awareness in space and time.

Make an obstacle more manageable by breaking it down into steps. When you break down obstacles into bite-sized steps, the situation doesn't feel as overwhelming anymore. Focus on what you can do instead of thinking about what you cannot do. Use the obstacle as a means to become better or think of creative ways to overcome it. When you hit a wall, find a way to climb it or build a hole in the wall to get to the other side. Don't just stand there and wonder why you hit the wall. Often, we assume our problems occur to hinder our progress, or that life is conspiring against us. The truth is, circumstances or events occurring in our lives have been called forth to help and guide us along our paths. Developing the right mindset is one of the best solutions for overcoming obstacles and achieving goals.

Obstacles are inevitable; all successful people have faced and overcome their own obstacles. The conviction of your goals, a smart plan, creative solutions, and the right mindset can give you a powerful determination to succeed. While you can't avoid obstacles, you can transform them into opportunities to become more resilient, skilled, and resourceful. You get to face who you really are during your toughest moments; do you want to be somebody who gets knocked out or someone who emerges stronger on the other side? Develop an unshakable belief in yourself and your abilities, and you will achieve any goal. When there is chaos in life, you need to focus on the process that can provide a way. This will help you deal with the situation without worrying about what might happen. When in doubt, just keep moving forward. Obstacles only appear when we take our focus off our goals. To turn your obstacles into opportunities, you need to perceive them as merely a detour. Your goal is achievable. Without obstacles, achieving anything would be easy, and without the struggle, there is no point in fighting for something you are aiming for. Instead of trying to fight it, try different methods of dealing with it.

Obstacles are put in our way to test whether or not what we want is worth fighting for. Often, we can become deterred by an obstacle and lose our way. Your mind instantly fears the challenge ahead of you and begins to self-doubt, and that alone is enough to defeat you. I remember taking a job with a New Jersey school system; it was a great job with good pay. I was a Desktop Support Technician; it was a good opportunity to work on my own and also work with some skilled IT folks. Because it was with the state of New Jersey, it had great benefits. I thought I had it made with this state job with great benefits, but after my first year, my position was eliminated. The school did not get the funding that it had anticipated and had to cut the budget which included non-teaching staff. So, I, of course, was the last one hired and the first one to be let go.

At first, I thought that I was going to be able to find a job right away, but two and three months started to go by, and I was not having any luck finding an IT job in New Jersey. I was very concerned. My parents had moved to North Carolina and I was living in New Jersey on my own, with rent, a car payment, and bills to pay. I spent months and months applying for jobs in New Jersey and New York City but not getting any luck in my industry. One of my cousins suggested that I seek opportunities in other states outside of New Jersey that had a higher demand for Information Technology specialists.

So, to make a long story short, about two years later, I landed a job in Washington, D.C. I would say that the timeframe from being laid off to finding a permanent job was a test of my strength and also a test to see who I could really depend on. I can see who my real friends were and who had my back. During that time, I managed to find some odd jobs to compensate and keep me from being evicted. I may have fallen behind on some bills, but I made just barely enough to pay my rent and my car payment, so I had a roof over my head and a car to drive to interviews or work.

So, this obstacle led me to bigger opportunities; you see, God will put you through something to get you ready for something bigger. Every path you choose has obstacles. Even if you have done everything in your power to avoid them, you will still end up facing them. That's because you need to confront them first to overcome them. Opportunities are usually disguised as obstacles to help us on our path. They can advance action by triggering emotion and improving your abilities. I often wonder what I would be doing now if I had stayed in New Jersey these last fifteen years. I don't think I would even be writing this book or be in this spiritual mindset that I have right now. I definitely wouldn't know the people that have crossed my path these last fifteen years.

What stands in your way is your way to achieve something. The obstacle in front of you has a purpose, and your mind learns to adapt to it and figure out a way around it. The struggles we face offer us a whole new perspective on growth and success.

So, to overcome your obstacles, focus on your strengths, not your weaknesses. If you replace a lack of ability in any area with determination, you will achieve any goal. When a crisis confronts you, the natural instinct is to think about your weaknesses. But instead of thinking about what you cannot do, think about what you can do. And that will be a game-changer. The first time we react to hardship in a different way is not easy, but in time we develop the habit of affirmative action, and in turn, our mental strength will increase. When we use our strengths, the accomplishment can motivate us and boost our progress at a faster pace. Think about the bigger picture; whatever you're thinking, think bigger!

Sometimes when we set goals, we are so focused on our problems that we hold ourselves back and miss out on the big picture. All successful people that have faced and overcome their obstacles had bigger goals in mind and a plan on how to get there. That makes all the difference. If you get frustrated while pursuing your goals, don't just complain and give up. That would only mean that you haven't pursued anything. All great accomplishments start by saying yes. Even if it is not completely to your liking or you don't feel ready, you need to get up and get started. Turn off the television, stop coming up with excuses, and stay away from distractions. If you have the will to take the first step, you will gain the momentum to keep moving forward, and your focus on the final outcome will keep you going through tough times. With this strategy, you will surely be successful in achieving your goals.

Chapter Twelve *Food for thought* on *Obstacles are your path to Opportunity*

What have you always wanted to do? What obstacles are stopping you from doing it?

How can you turn your situation into an opportunity?

CHAPTER 13

Family Ties

When I wrote this book, I wanted to make sure that it would empower whoever is reading the book to do better in life. Being better in life also means knowing how to deal with family on so many different levels, from your father, mother, siblings and extended family members, such as grandparents, uncles, aunts, cousins, and in-laws. I grew up with great parents; both my father and mother took care of my brother and me. I grew up in a house where both my parents took part in raising my brother and me and were a part of our everyday life.

As you go through life, no matter what personal issues you are going through, your parents are always going to be there. Your family is always there. You don't get to change them; they will always be there. You can unfriend friends and not be someone's friend, but family will always be there. From the time that I was a young child, I was always told who my immediate family members and extended family members were (grandparents, aunts, uncles, and cousins). I was always told who and how people are related to me, and I think it is important for children to know who their family members are. They should be able to sketch out a simple family tree of their parents, grandparents, aunts, uncles and cousins.

Family is the single most important influence in a child's life. From their first moments of life, children depend on parents and family to protect them and provide for their needs. Parents and families form a child's first relationships. They are a child's first teachers and act as role models in how to act and how to experience the world around them. Children thrive when parents actively promote their positive growth and development. My parents were always supportive of anything my brother and I wanted to do. When I was middle school age, I wanted to attend modeling school, and my parents supported me in that effort. Now, I didn't become America's top model, but I learned a lot from attending modeling school, such as etiquette, how to walk with confidence and how to apply makeup.

My brother wanted to play on the football team at an early age, and my parents supported him. It's important that parents support their children's aspirations. As we got older, they continued to support our interests. They were always there for us. As I was growing up, I was able to know my paternal grandmother, and I watched how my father and his siblings would come together on her behalf and make plans to take care of her. I recall one time when my father and his siblings gathered together in their home state of North Carolina to meet and discuss care for my paternal grandmother.

My father had six siblings, and they came together without arguing and fighting and discussed how they would care for their mother as she was getting older and needed a caretaker. My grandmother needed someone to come in a few hours during the week and prepare meals, clean the house and keep her company. All of my grandmother's children except for one lived outside of the state where she lived, so they needed to discuss care for their mother, and there was no doubt that all seven siblings were on the same page when it came to the love and care of their mother. They came up with a monthly fee that each sibling would pay, and this lasted until my grandmother passed at ninety-four years old. This to me was setting an example for your children to see you taking care of your parents as they got older. Children watch their parents, and I was watching mine, so when my parents got older, I knew to take care of them, which is what we are supposed to do. They took care of us when we were babies and until we were at least twenty-one years old. It's life, and it shouldn't be hard to figure out, but it's good when a child can witness the process in a civil manner.

Honor your parents; that's what I was taught at a very young age, and watching my father and his siblings take care of their mother was one example I observed. As a child, I had to obey my parents and listen to what they told me to do. As I got older, I didn't always listen, and in some cases, I regretted not listening. Perhaps the most important way we can honor our parents is to forgive them. The fact is, there are no perfect parents. If you have experienced a situation with your parents, you need to forgive them and move on, because holding on to that will not solve anything or help the situation.

When I hear some of my friends mention that they aren't speaking to their mom or dad for whatever reason, I just don't understand. I currently have one living parent and would do anything just to speak to or see my dad again. Some of your parents have made unwise decisions, they have had unrealistic expectations, or they have said and done things that have left us deeply wounded. For that reason, many of you enter adulthood controlled by anger and bitterness. You find that you're unable to move past your parents' mistakes or your parents' sins. Just forgive them and move on. Things may not be what they use to be, but it will help you move forward. One of the best things to do is to honor our parents.

Another way we can honor our parents is to speak well of them, to refuse to speak evil of them. We need to speak well of them while they are alive and speak well of them after they have died, to speak well of them to our siblings, to our spouses, to our children and the rest of the family. We also honor our parents when we seek their wisdom through life's twists and turns. We do well, then, to lean on them for understanding, to seek their input when faced with major decisions. It honors our parents when we seek their help, even if in the end we cannot or must not heed it. We are to support them and help provide for them in their old age; children need to reassure their parents that they will be taken care of.

It's important to get together with family on happy occasions and not just for funerals because it gives family members a chance to connect, have fun, and get to know each other. The children get to know their cousins and create memories. Sometimes coming together was a trip to Grandmas, and those trips were priceless. Every time I would visit my Grandmother, she would tell me stories and history about the family. When my grandmother passed, my Aunt Bernice would also tell me the history of the family on my paternal side and my Uncle Joe would tell me the family history on my maternal side. All these connections helped build relationships with family members, and learning the history also inspired me to dig further into family history from a geological perspective. I can say that I am one of those cousins that knows most of the family; the one that someone will call to ask who's who and how we are connected. Overall, connecting with family has established very close friendships through relationships built with my cousins at various ages.

Sometimes when a family begins to mature, that potential loss of connection, that feeling of something changing, is difficult to confront. When the siblings begin to have their own families and everyone lives in different cities and states, sometimes it's hard to reconnect to family members as they begin to grow. My grandmother used to say, "Keep my family together." So as time has gone by, we have lost some of the patriarchs and matriarchs of the family, and get-togethers have become fewer and fewer. I'm hoping that my family will come together soon as we are maturing and there are new generations blossoming.

As families mature and grow, there are ways to stay in touch. Keep the lines open; learn ways to communicate with family members. Some may stay in touch by texting, and for some it may just be a phone call or even social media. You may not be able to visit often, but if you can, you should try to visit the senior family members. Sometimes they feel as though they are forgotten when family doesn't visit them.

Family can be complicated and sometimes a little dysfunctional when other factors come into play. One thing you want to try to stay away from is family gossip. Gossip is very damaging. Most often, gossip occurs when someone is upset by something related to the person they are gossiping about. Family should be a person's first source for love, acceptance, and support. Unfortunately, many extended families are failing miserably as the people within the family do things to undercut family unity. Understanding the problem is the first step in finding a solution. I'll admit I have been guilty of receiving gossip about family members. Now when that happens, I usually speak to the person privately and find out what is going on and why they are spreading this information. If you have a problem or issue with someone in the family, then go to them directly. You don't need to announce your issue in front of the whole family. Some people do this to force family members to choose sides in a situation. When sides are taken, there is a divide in the family. Instead, go privately to that person with whom you have a problem. Discuss the issues, but do so with the goal of reconciliation.

Insults and criticism: words carry weight, and in some cases, they can carry the weight of the world. When unkind words are said to family, they hurt. Your family is supposed to be your source of encouragement and support. Negative words damage the core of family relationships. Some family members may say things off the cuff and think that because these things were said casually, they don't hurt the other person. When negative words are spoken to family members, it creates a coldness in the relationship. It takes time and positive interactions to repair the harm that is done when insults and criticisms take place.

Inclusion of family members is essential to family unity. Include all family members at family functions such as family reunions. Even if you know they are going to say no, ask anyway. Now, if you have a large family, sometimes everyone cannot attend weddings and events when one person is footing the bill, unlike something like a family reunion or family event where all family members are pitching in and making an effort towards the contributions. Some family members catch hard feelings because of failure to ask and failure to include. Deception in a family is destructive. The truth always prevails; sometimes it may take years or even a generation for the lies and deceit to become known, but know that they will come to light someday. Lying to family or using deception to keep secrets leads to brokenness in a family. This brokenness comes from trust being corroded. The bigger the lie, the bigger the corrosion.

Your actions have consequences, not just to you, but to your extended family for generations to come. It is much better to admit your wrongdoings and work toward healing than to lie and work to carry that lie around indefinitely or until you are found out. Just because you come from the same parents doesn't mean you will be the same, or if you have the same grandparents, it doesn't mean your siblings will be the same or do the same things. Allow others to be different. Just because you are family doesn't mean you have to share the same political views or even the same religion. People will grow up and have different parenting styles and lifestyle choices, but it is not the job of family members to judge. Love and acceptance start in the family. Accept people for who they are and for where they are in life. Acceptance of a person for who they are is the ultimate form of love.

Any relationship can be resolved with apologies and forgiveness, but the hurt can still remain long after harsh words are exchanged. Be careful with your words. Remind yourself that as family, you are there to be one another's greatest supporters in life. Tearing others in the family down with words is destructive to the family unit. Apologies and forgiveness is the glue that keeps a family together. Nobody is perfect. At some point in time, you will hurt a member of the family. It is up to you to say the words, "I am sorry," for whatever the case may be. Those words can heal wounds and create a stronger family bond. When you apologize to a family member, the message you are sending to the person is that they matter and that you don't want ill feelings between you and them. Not apologizing is sending the message that the person does not matter or that their feelings don't matter. Be the bigger person and apologize when you do something wrong against a family member; whether your words or actions that hurt the person were intentional or not, it does not matter. What matters is that the apology takes place. You can explain intentions, but you can't make someone "un-feel" being wronged.

One thing I try to do with my cousins, especially the ones that are younger than me, is to give them positive feedback if they share something with me. I will always keep it real and honest, but I wouldn't want to insult them. My cousins are amazing, and they are from all walks of life and are doing a lot of great things in the world. We are not perfect, and I don't have the perfect family. We have had ups and downs, but ultimately, we always have each other's back.

"Family is the lock and togetherness is the key."

Chapter Thirteen *Food for thought* on Family Ties

What do you like the most about your family?

Are you in conflict with anyone in your family (ex: parent, sibling, cousin, etc..)? How are you working to resolve the issue?

Epilogue

I hope after reading my book, you will develop a sense that nothing can stop you. I am not perfect and don't expect to be. But I try every day to be the best Taunya I can be. I don't want to be like anyone else; I am Taunya Lynnette and the one any only. I have not done anything to myself that is artificial; I am one hundred percent real, and when my friends or family ask me a question, they know they are getting the truth. I hope this book is able to help you get through this thing called life, from building up your confidence and having the self-esteem to doing anything life throws at you.

I hope that you can encourage yourself and not wait for someone to encourage you. Sometimes your friends and family won't be around, so you have to be able to encourage yourself. I hope that whatever it is you were afraid of, you are no longer afraid because you know that fear fails. Do not let fear hold you back; get out of your comfort zone and live life. You can stand up for what you believe in. You are brave, bold, and beautiful enough to be afraid to try something, but do it anyway. You know that you may experience stress from time to time, but you also know when it's too much, and you are familiar with symptoms of stress and will seek help if needed.

Just being you is turning your obstacles into opportunities and focusing on your strengths, not your weaknesses, with self-determination. When you thought you had a problem, you now have an opportunity. God will turn it around—keep the faith!

I hope that if you haven't done so by now that you will invest in yourself. Learn a new skill; don't just dream of doing something, but live it. Take the classes you need to take things to the next level, and stop making up excuses. Invest in yourself, whether it is to improve your skills at work or your personal life. Don't wait or depend on others to live out your dreams.

When things are going great, life will throw you a curveball and hit you hard with the death of a loved one or close friend. Death will come. We are going to lose the ones we love eventually; no one will live forever. You will have grief, and it will be rough at times, but things will get better. You will always have the memory of your loved one, and they would not want you to self-destruct or stop living your best life because they are not here. Find someone to talk to about your grief if it comes to that. You may have to seek a therapist if needed. Grief is a part of life; what's important is how you can recover and move on with your life.

Your body is your temple; you are what you eat. If you start to notice something wrong with your body, you must get it checked out. Don't wait month after month, because it could mean life or death, a cure, or six months to live. You know your body, and if something isn't right with it, follow your instincts and see a doctor.

Remember, friends make us who we are when we choose the right ones. A real friend is one who walks in when the rest of the world walks out. A real, true friend listens to you. A real friend is honest and not jealous of you. Friendship is a relationship of enjoyment and convenience; you choose who you want to be your friend.

EPILOGUE

Family is forever. You don't have a choice; you were born into it. Tell someone in your family that you love them. Don't wait until they are gone to give them flowers or say what's on your mind. Try to find a way to stay connected to your family; don't lose touch, and don't lose the history.

Like I mentioned in previous chapters, become unbreakable, create personal resilience, be unstoppable! We cannot escape pain, difficulty, failure, tragedy, and heartache. Sooner or later it will find us, despite our best efforts to protect ourselves. Now, as you are becoming unbreakable, you can be unstoppable and successful all at the same time!

Just be yourself. I'm just being me.

Acknowledgments

Thank you, God, for without you, I am nothing. Thank you to my parents, to my mother Earnestine, I love you! To my father Ernest, you may be gone physically, but you are not forgotten. Although you are no longer with us, I love you and truly miss you. Thank you to my big brother Ernest Jr.; I love you for always having my back, we may not see eye to eye sometimes but no matter what you are always looking out for your little sister. To my sister-in-love, Donna, I love you and thank you for loving my brother.

Thank you to my church, First Baptist Church of Glenarden (FBCG), under the leadership of Pastor John K. Jenkins Sr. and First Lady Trina Jenkins, for the teachings and providing a place of worship and developing dynamic disciples. It was through the ministries of FBCG where I have met some amazing women of God and where my spiritual growth really began from Divine Discipleship of Sisters (DDS), The Bible Institutes & Focus Studies classes. Thank you for giving me the opportunity to let my light shine using my gift of writing. It was in DDS where I wrote my first article for their quarterly newsletters, and as I continue to serve in writing inspirational articles for women, by women with *Grace Magazine* in the Women's Ministry, I pray that the words that I say will inspire them to be a better person.

Thank you to my mentor, Tressa Azarel Smallwood, for your encouragement; you are a great teacher and friend. I am so blessed to have connected with you and your VIP Club. If it weren't for your course, "Write and Publish Like a Pro," I would not have finished this book. Your VIP Club has connected me with so many amazing people, from authors and writers to film and TV producers and directors. You are a Diamond in the rough, and if they don't know who you are, they will soon find out!

Thank you to my family and friends for your love, support, and encouragement.

Peace & blessings,
Taunya

About the Author

Taunya is a writer, photographer, world traveler, and child of God. Taunya Lynnette amazes the world as she tells stories through words and photos. She's a creative writer who not only writes stories but also inspires women. Some of her inspirational work can be found in *Grace Magazine*, a publication written by women, for women. Taunya also provides photography services for portraits, illustrations, fashion, sports, small events and everything in between.

By day, Taunya is a skilled Cyber Security professional with over twenty years of experience in various disciplines of information technology, network and system administration, security operations, information assurance, computer incident response and cybersecurity awareness and training within federal, state and local government as well as the private sector. In a field where women are few, Taunya has overcome some of the toughest obstacles, in most cases, as the only woman and often having to prove herself to others in a male-dominated field.

Taunya is passionate about writing stories and allowing the stories to be seen through photography. She is a creative by nature and also creates content that can be used for television and film. Taunya empowers women through words, and during her off time, she loves traveling around the world, listening to music, and spending time with family and friends. Taunya is a native of East Orange, New Jersey and currently resides in the Washington, D.C. Metropolitan area.

Made in the USA
Middletown, DE
22 June 2024

56152975R10073